Quilt University

Quilt University
Transforming Oral Learning Into Academic Knowledge

Lucy Thelma Osbourne, M.Ed.

Afterword by Lynne Hamer, Ph.D.

2013

 QU Press

Toledo, Ohio

Copyright (c) 2013 by Lucy Thelma Osbourne, M.Ed.
Afterword copyright (c) 2013 by Lynne Hamer, Ph.D.

Cover Photo of University of Toledo clock tower: Daniel Miller, courtesy of University of Toledo Marketing

Quilts pictured are from a collection owned by Ethel Waddell; photos by Lynne Hamer.

All rights reserved. No part of this book may be reproduced or utilized in any form or by any means, electronic or mechanical, including photocopying, recording, or by any information storage and retrieval system, without permission in writing from the publisher.

Printed in the United State of America

Library of Congress Cataloging-in-Publication Data
Osbourne, Lucy Thelma
Quilt university /
Lucy Thelma Osbourne, —1st ed.

ISBN: 0615710425
ISBN-13: 9780615710426 (pbk.) Lucy Thelma Osbourne

Acknowledgements

I begin with acknowledging the support of my children: Nep Brassfield, Chay Brassfield, Iva Brassfield, and Joy Osbourne.

A special shout out to my grandson Anthony Holland, Jr. He inspired this project a long time ago when I asked him what I should write about. He replied, "Grandma, write about you. That would be the most interesting subject I can think of."

Granddaughter Jordyn Goodner asked the questions and helped me to get the words right. Julia and Samantha Hamer-Light made profound statements that gave me food for thought.

Thanks to grandchildren Candace and Akil Jones, and their children Legaci and A.J., and to granddaughter Giavanna (Gigi), and her children London, Heiress, and King, who were on board for the push of this literary work.

To Dr. Tom Barden, Dr. Abbie Robinson-Armstrong, and Dr. Paddy Bowman, my extensive gratitude for their helpful reviews and for encouraging me to publish. To Dr. Lynne Hamer, for her professional and personal dedication to this project, from the beginning to the editing of the book, I extend an immeasurable thank you for her investment of time and commitment.

To my niece Cynthia Lee and my lifelong friend Bess Fletcher, thank you for your moral support. To my cousin Ethel Waddell, thank you for keeping and sharing the family quilts.

To all the other family and friends who have encouraged me in many and different ways, thank you. Even though I cannot mention you all by name, my heart remains appreciative for your support.

I must take time to thank the University of Toledo for allowing me to have a space to express ideas and personal experiences, as well as its marketing department for design of the cover and help with the layout of the book.

Contents

PIECE 1:	Introduction	1
PIECE 2:	Learning Environments	5
PIECE 3:	Early Thoughts	9
PIECE 4:	What Is a Quilt?	11
PIECE 5:	Crazy Quilt	19
PIECE 6:	Patchwork Quilt	25
PIECE 7:	Home and School	29
PIECE 8:	My Grandfather	37

PIECE 9:	Experience and Education	39
PIECE 10:	Cut Off from Book Knowledge	43
PIECE 11:	Entering Academic University	47
PIECE 12:	Quilting Frames and Theoretical Frames	55
PIECE 13:	Community in Quilt University and Lack of Community in Academic University	61
PIECE 14:	The Quilt Connection	69
PIECE 15:	Call-And-Response in Quilt University and Academic University	73
PIECE 16:	Missing Pieces/Finding Pieces	79
PIECE 17:	Why Life Stories of Quilters?	83

PIECE 18:	Quilting History: Harriet Powers	87
PIECE 19:	Quilting As Connecting: Renee Walton	91
PIECE 20:	Quilting As Process: Alice Walker	97
PIECE 21:	Zora Neale Hurston	101
PIECE 22:	Conclusion: Piecing Society	105

Afterword: Piecing as Democratic Pedagogy
by Lynne Hamer   115

Works Cited   127

The Nancy Evans & Allie Grace Quilt Collection, 1930 – 1958

Quilts made by Nancy Evans and Allie Grace from the 1930s through the 1950s and pictured throughout this book are from the collection of Ethel Waddell. Lucy Thelma Osbourne is Nancy Evans's granddaughter and Allie Grace's daughter, and Ethel Waddell is their niece.

PIECE 1

Introduction

Quilt University is my metaphor for a learning environment where people meet to validate themselves while establishing a community in which they practice learning. I use the quilt to chronicle my experience as a non-traditional African American graduate student participating in an academic learning environment. I had already raised a family of four children and they had completed college before I went to the University of Toledo for my bachelor's degree. I continued straight on into a Master of Education degree which I completed at age 71, and went directly on to pursue coursework towards two additional master's degrees. In completing my Master of Education degree, I "pieced my thesis." That is, I used my own way of assembling knowledge (pieces) to make a work that was meaningful to me (a quilt), but that also fulfilled institutional requirements for the degree. Thus instead of chapters, in that thesis and in this book, I have "pieces." The issues I encountered in this learning experience and process raised some significant questions that motivated the metaphors "Quilt University" and "Academic University."

Throughout my life I have participated in both Quilt University and Academic University, and both are important to me for different reasons. Quilt University is important because this is where I get a sense of value, identity, and connection to community, family, and culture, and where I learn survival skills necessary to participate in everyday life. Academic University is important because that is where I get information to be able to live successfully in society. One of my colleagues asked me why I wanted to write about women of color. I told her it was because that is who I am and I am looking for a way to know myself. If I don't know my past or how I got to where I am now, then I do not exist. Academic literature reviews could not define who I am because I am not in the writing—and they do not know me, either. With my work in these pages I begin to fill a gap in the literature that I read.

I ask, What can I learn from quilters Harriet Powers, Renee Walton, Alice Walker, and Zora Neale Hurston? In different ways and to different degrees, each of these women used her home in Quilt University to move successfully into Academic University. In order for me to get into the system, I needed to understand the past and what brought me to this work. Those outside the institution—the women in this book—had to learn to trust their inner voices. For two of them (Powers and Walton), those inner voices came through making quilts; for one (Walker), inner voice came through quilting and writing; and for the fourth (Hurston), inner voice came from participation in community

INTRODUCTION

through stories. The dominant culture—outside voices including those in Academic University—can keep you on the outside by not accepting your base of knowledge. If individuals are to survive in the dominant culture and in Academic University, they need to rely on their inner voices and trust themselves and the universe as centers from which to speak, identify, and validate self.

I thus use the metaphors of Quilt University and Academic University to compare and contrast the learning which takes place in informal settings, such as quilting groups, with that which takes place in formal, academic learning environments. In doing so, I focus on how significant quilts are in learning about the history of women's lives, specifically women of color. I ask, What is the relationship of the quilt to women's lives, mine included? What can be learned from bits and pieces of data based on quilt culture? How can I piece the lives of the women included in this work to create a center to understand simultaneous participation in Quilt University and Academic University—participation without assimilation, i.e., without giving up one to participate in the other?

Lucy Thelma Osbourne, Toledo, Ohio, 2012

PIECE 2

Learning Environments

In my experience there are two key learning environments, one inside the established academic institutions of learning, and the other in everyday life situations. Theories in the field of Folklore and Education are useful in bringing clarity to these different learning processes. White and Congdon (1998) tell us:

> Students learn as they bring their own traditional (folk) inquiry together with the academic (fine) inquiry that exists in schools. Learning may be defined by the success that students develop in negotiating the relationships between these two realms. This negotiation involves continual defining and redefining of who we are and what we do, which is in essence a "state of social reconstruction." (p. 41)

My chronicle of Quilt University is intended to provide a sort of pattern or map for others wishing to negotiate their relationships between these two realms, and to live successfully in both.

In Quilt University, the curriculum begins with group participation in oral storytelling, during the piecing and sewing, in which different participants put out different subjects: church happenings, politics, a wedding or some other important event that will soon take place. The topic that the most people agree upon becomes the topic of the day. The quilting process continues by cutting scraps of fabric into pieces and stitching them together to complete the quilt pattern. As each piece is cut and stitched, a different story is being told—and it is told from the perspective of whose dress scrap, or whose pajama scrap, or whose piece of choir robe is being cut and stitched. These stories are the knowledge, the memories, which become encoded into the piece of fabric, and combined with other pieces into the curriculum of the quilt. Thus anybody participating in the stitching knows the stories, has mastered the curriculum, and accesses that knowledge every time she looks at the completed quilt. *This was Aunt Ida's dress that she wore to church the day of the revival. The other women admired that dress and how pretty it was. That was during the Depression, when the government rationed fabric and you were lucky to get yours off a pretty bolt or to be able to get enough flour sacks of the same pattern to make a dress.* Not only can the quilter recall the knowledge, but she passes it on to others who use the quilt down through the years.

Key in this process is the connection between the stories told in the quilting, the patterns, the fabric, and the participants. Folklorist Barbara Kirshenblatt-Gimblett (1983) names these women "indigenous teachers," and she urges educators to bring indigenous teachers' knowledge and pedagogy into classrooms. My indigenous teachers taught so much more than could be learned reading texts. In the oral process stories were told to create quilted texts by identifying people and events as the fabric in the quilt. The stories were read orally by the people who participated in the quilt making.

My work here demonstrates how the knowledge from Quilt University can be pieced together to become written text and therefore recognized as valid knowledge in Academic University. Throughout my undergraduate and graduate careers, what surfaced on the inside of the academic institution and outside of it were two different learning styles. I had to negotiate the relationship between the knowledge I brought and the knowledge I encountered. I see the different learning styles in terms of the crazy quilt, in which the pattern of the quilt is not apparent in the beginning of the work but emerges in the end, and the patchwork quilt, in which the pattern is determined in the beginning and changes very little in the end.

When I wrote my master's thesis, I used quilt pieces instead of chapters to piece my thesis together. The basis for this was that Quilt University is where my indigenous teachers taught quilt making and at the same time dealt with issues from a context of survival. These teachers taught so much more than could be learned reading text. In the oral process stories were told to create quilt text by identifying people and events as the fabric in the quilt. The stories were read orally by the people who participated in the quilt making.

Quilt University represents a world that is outside the mainstream institution. It is a place to connect bits and pieces of knowledge—to attempt connecting with the established norms of learning and at the same time to validate self and place self at the center of learning. Academic University creates a learning environment based on a prescribed, written curriculum. I quilt my writing as a way to connect the two different learning environments. In so doing, I can take oral texts that are known to me and place them in written form to be used in academic learning. My work therefore demonstrates that knowledge from Quilt University can be pieced together to become written text recognizable as valid knowledge in Academic University.

PIECE 3

Early Thoughts

There is an interdisciplinary aspect to quilt ideology. Quilting includes history, politics, art, anthropology, sociology, education, communication, and interpersonal relationships. These data are stored in someone's memory and can be accessed through storytelling and oral history. Would there be information in these stories that would give educators more insight to learning if these data were available to them?

Quilt stories are by and in large women's stories. I am especially interested in women's stories because we have been excluded from full participation in the education process. Black women have been left out of the educational processes because of the way they have been placed in history and at times omitted from participation in their educations because of the way curricula are crafted: Not about us. Black women more than any other women are left out.

Further, what can the stories tell us about how these women were able to struggle and survive the conditions in their lives? How did they use quilting to stitch and hold their lives together and make meaning? Was quilting A WAY TO RESIST OPPRESSION AND THE ROLES THEY HAD BEEN ASSIGNED TO PLAY in a society that does not provide an equal opportunity for them to participate from a position of power (white) rather than from a position of oppression (black). How can the oppressed group participate from a position of equality when there are two processes involved? I hope the quilt stories here will give some insight into the lives of these women to help them connect to a body of information that is different from their own inside/outside participation in a community of learners. The quilting community of practice is different from the academic community of practice. The quilt stories come from an oral community of learning. Academic learning involves text and curriculum and is written down. Can they connect and learn from each other? On the one hand, lack of education and capital has been a barrier to participation in higher learning. On the other hand, if there were no new knowledge to access orally, where would academia get information to write down? Knowledge is not good or bad, just different. Lave and Wenger's (1991) concept of "situated learning" provides a framework useful in bridging the gap between folklore theory (language) and educational practice. Lave and Wenger contribute the notion "that learning is a way of being in the social world, not a way of coming to know about it."

PIECE 4

What Is a Quilt?

A quilt is not just an old blanket to keep you warm. When viewed with respect, a quilt has many meanings. As I consider my personal experience as well as scholarship on quilts, I see the quilt as many things. Among other things, it is a historical document, a coded text, a cultural artifact, and an institution.

First, a quilt is history. Through the study of quilts, historians have traced the cultural influences of African cultures on American cultures. Using quilts as historical documents, we learn:

> Quilts were developed in Africa as far back as two thousand years, when cotton was domesticated along the Niger River in Mali. Quilts were used for fishnet and woven cloth. The actual links between African and African-American textile

> traditions can be traced to the years between 1650 and 1850 when Africans were brought to Latin America, the Caribbean and the United States. African influence on American Folk Art such as quilt making is less well known than Euro-American quilt making. (Wahlman, 1993, p. 55)

Thus quilts serve as primary sources in recovering and restitching the history of a people.

Second, a quilt is also a text. Studying quilts from another angle, linguists have noted how quilts are used as texts for communication:

> African-American quilting is a unique art form with its own history and meaning that exists within a cultural context. The quilt represents more than an art form. They represent a way of life and unity for a people misplaced in an environment that processed them from a different context established by a dominant cultural ideology. African-American quilts can be read as texts and contain secret codes for a people in a hostile environment. These codes were used to survive in a New World that did not allow freedom to express and create a place to move upward in the established systems and institutions. (Wahlman, 1993, pp. 51-52)

The quilt as text is also an image made by women to be used as an oral text to herself or her closest friends. Elsley (1996) describes the quilt as this sort of text:

> It speaks the language of its maker's desires and beliefs, hopes, and fears, sometimes in a language any reader can understand, but often in an obscure language available only to the initiated. Quilts and texts are inseparable. The quilt can be read as an oral text that has not been analyzed and interpreted. (p. xx)

In creating my written text, I piece my data. Scraps of leftover materials and ideas are used to create the patterns, using original, intuitive imagination in order to stitch together thoughts from a fabric that is returned to again and again. This fabric is read as data in the quilts; it is also data in my written text.

Third, a quilt is a cultural artifact. The quilt has functioned throughout history to keep people together while serving as a way to tie them together, and a cultural focal point around which they gathered to share experiences and celebrations about family and community. Women not only told stories; quilt gatherings were also places where they could return again and again to form community, get a sense of self, and share everyday experiences while they collaborated in a form of learning. The stories told at quilt gatherings got passed down from generation to generation in an oral tradition by reading the fabric and designs to associate it with a time and a place. Elsley (1993) observes:

> When people are not permitted to celebrate their traditional ceremonies, speak their own language, or pass on their customs to their children, they do not relinquish these ideas, they just change the code so the oppressors cannot recognize what they are doing. Quilts were a way where powerless people could empower themselves to communicate, express, and create meaning by stitching their thoughts, ideas, and issues in fabric, using symbolic designs to visually present their messages to a group where they could be accessed orally from their memory. (p. 116)

Quilts are important in Quilt University. As one woman said, "A quilt serves as an apt metaphor for stitching together our ragged world" (Elsley, 1996, p. 65). The patchwork quilt is really a symbol of the world which must come. One new design made of many old designs. We will stitch this world together yet. Don't give up.

Fourth, a quilt is an institution with its own discourse. Quilt University is an institution created by women of color who did not have an opportunity to participate in the institution of Academic University where emphasis is placed on the written word. Multivocality is one very important and powerful department in Quilt University because that is where everyone gets to speak and the speech gets accepted and validated, as authentic parts of Quilt University and making individual speakers authentic members of Quilt University. A variety of subjects surface in this collaborative classroom where each student brings bits and pieces of scraps and ideas from their area of concern to be talked about and to get a group consensus as to how these patterns should be stitched together to make a quilt.

The quilt is crafted in Quilt University as the process of learning actually takes place and the data are processed and recorded in memory. Quilt University is a place where quilt makers return again and again to access data visually and to use it in creative processes, recording history, connecting to the past, writing books in fabric. Elsley (1993) notes:

> Quilting is quiet, meditative work. The quilter centers on the regular, rocking movement of the needle, feeling the subtle ridges of the cotton from under her fingers. She focuses on her needle, her fingers, her thread, her breathing and the detail of the quilt. Quilting is tactile, sensual, spiritual work. (p. 23)

Group quilters give insights in the growing intimacy that takes place in the institution of Quilt University. The inward motion draws the quilters, as well as the quilt, together by a common thread that establishes friendship and emotional support. In 1948, quilt historian Elizabeth Wells Robertson gave this description of what we can call a discourse community of quilters:

> When twelve women arranged three on a side of the quilt frame started out to quilt, they were wide apart: Indeed they were nine feet apart. But as the sides were rolled up, they came closer and closer together until, when the quilt was finished, they were face to face. The conversation would be very general when the quilt started—the crops and the weather were safe subjects, also politics, which, as we see, actually entered into the names of some quilts. At first the talk was loud enough to be heard by all but as the quilters came closer and closer together, the conversation became correspondingly more intimate. (Quoted in Elsley, 1996, p. 55)

This way of relating to each other and to knowledge—that is, the discourse—is recognized by others as well. The great creator of written texts, Alice Walker, is also a creator of quilts. Patricia Hill Collins (1990) cited Walker as asserting:

> The process of quilting helps women to join with each other. Sewing/stitching is one way to begin the process of reclaiming self because it represents power and a symbol of connection. What is needed is the appreciation of art, of life in a larger perspective. Connections made, or attempted where none existed before, the straining to encompass in one's glance at the varied world of common thread, the unifying theme of immense diversity. (p. 238)

WHAT IS A QUILT?

Similarly, quilt scholars Ferrero, Hedges, and Silber (1987) noted of quilters that "as they became closer and more trusting [the women] dealt with intimate issues that could not be spoken publicly. The common thread that bound the quilt together gave a place where women could give and receive emotional support. It gave women of color a place for cultural cohesion" (p. 63). Quilt University gave groups of women a gathering place outside the patriarchy of men.

Quilting can be seen as participatory, collaborative learning experience. Black feminist literary theorist Patricia Hill Collins (1990) described this as follows:

> One 23-year old woman of color, who participated in a community education project, tells us: "I learned so much more than I could ever learn in the classroom. I learned that there is a whole lot more than getting a degree and getting ahead financially. You must do so with dignity and principle. You can't sit back and watch all the atrocities continue to happen, take your little class notes, read your books and do nothing to change conditions.

A type of community education, quilting groups were and are a safe place for women because they received no outside resistance from men. This made the quilting sessions a gathering place outside of the patriarchy.

Belonging to a community gives women a sense of self for the reason they are bonded through the quilt group. Dealing from a cultural context this is significant because it gives women a place to develop coping skills and to connect with other women. It is within this context of community that women discover individual power from the support they receive. Poet and theorist Audre Lorde (1984) saw the community as nurturing the individual woman . In her famous "Master's Tools" speech and essay, she observed that there exists a "paradox of individuality within community for women, articulating the desire to nurture each other is not pathological but redemptive, and it is within that knowledge that our real power is discovered" (1984, p. 111). Research shows that quilting groups process a close ongoing relationship between women of color. The meshing of ego boundaries reflects a social construct from the context of culture that is secure and empowering.

Quilts are thus valued in many ways besides being something to keep you warm. In his historical work on quilting, In his historical work on quilting, Freeman (1996) reported that the author Alice Walker finds "the quilt is important to her when she wants to write a book. She collects scraps, needles and thread and heads for a cabin in the woods. Quilt making enables her to create characters for her books. She tells us a rebirth of her memory occurs through piecing the quilt together" (p. 149). Quilts are used as a communion with self, where the individual retreats to access knowledge. This notion of individual quilters and how they use quilts to construct self and gain knowledge from inside in order to tell stories or write books is the central focus of my work.

PIECE 5

Crazy Quilt

The learning that takes place in Quilt University is best represented by the metaphor of the crazy quilt. In making a crazy quilt, quilters start out with no preset plan or pattern. Each quilter brings the scraps of fabric, ideas, and stories to the quilting session. Scraps of fabric are put together because they are the leftover materials that are available—pieced together randomly, without regard for color, pattern, texture, or size. When the quilt is complete, however, a pattern has been formed: the quilt is complete and aesthetically pleasing. Similarly, the quilters bring their ideas and stories to share during the quilting activity. All tell their stories, and as a group they coalesce around one story that emerges as the topic for the day. As they continue, each quilter adds her story and ideas, and by the time the quilt is completed, a new understanding of the topic -a new story-has emerged. When the quilters look at the completed quilt, they recall the completed story.

Furthermore, they can each identify their particular pieces of the quilt and the story. The story is not written down; it is stitched in the quilt, to be read orally. Neither the quilt nor its story is, in the end, random or nonsensical. It only appears "crazy" to those who are not trained to read it. As Elsley (1994) observed:

> "Crazy" is just one of the labels patriarchal society attaches to women it doesn't understand, women who won't fit in, or who refuse to play the masculine game. But [any so-called crazy woman] is not so crazy. She speaks a wild wisdom, which, while it does not coincide with linear reasoning, does show a profound understanding of a way of being for the many women who have spent their lives being marginalized by a culture that used women for its own convenience. Nothing can be sole or whole that has not been rent.
>
> A woman makes the world her own by taking apart the patriarchal ways of being to create a space for herself. That space allows her to accept her own fragmentation, embrace those fragments, and thus validate herself. Recognizing rather than denying her pieces is often a woman's way to becoming "sole or whole" in a more feminocentric way. (pp. 68-69)

A woman creates sense by asserting that wholeness is composed of that which is not fragments. A woman makes the world her own by creating a space for herself. Rearranging rather than denying her pieces is sometimes a way to become whole. Quilting gives a context for being creative which may be seen as an act of courage, necessity, and faith. Quilting also helps women to join with each other and network to support each other.

All of us in academia, especially those involved in feminist studies, are quilt making a space for ourselves in order to gather up our fragments into the construction of a pattern of our own liking. Elsley (1994) elaborated:

> Multi-pattern and multicolored, stitched by women from various racial and national cultures with various critical pre-dispositions a crazy quilt story can jump back and forth in time and work in different levels of the mind. This may be why literary writers Toni Morrison, Alice Walker, and Bell Hooks rely on quilt text when they reach a barrier in creating characters in written text. The quilt is an ideal artifact for interpretation and analyzing data because it's inclusive of the spectrum of experience for African-American women. Some educators go back in time, which the crazy quilt exemplifies, and start quilting to complete their lives. (p. 83)

As the educators reflect on a significant person in their lives, and they start the quilt process from a childhood context. This crazy quilt helps to hold together the survival skills to include everyone in the quilt. Different people return to the crazy quilt to identify and associate the pieces with someone important in their lives: "See this little piece that was Aunt Emma's dress that she wore to church on the Easter Sunday and I sat beside her." Another quilter might identify a piece as the one that "Grandma wore to Ann's wedding last summer"; another a piece as "the dress Momma wore the day she took me to school."

It is significant that the women Elsley (1994) quoted are college educated and taught school in mainstream institutions. They turned to quilting when they retired, which makes for an interesting analysis of the quilt text. Why do women want to return to a time to remember when an artifact had deep-felt meaning in the lives of the makers, participants, and observers? Could this be a time marker to allow women to connect the bits and pieces of data in their lives to complete a holistic process of self?

The crazy quilt is not crazy in the sense that it creates intricate structural solutions to effect unity from great variety. Hilliard (1994) described:

> As a collage, quilts are an emblem of rhetorical action of assembling old forms to create new, dialectical sought wholes. Crazy quilts were, in effect, metaphors of concise-diverse elements agreeing to interact and hold together, to coexist for a synthetic, greater good. (p. 123)

Quilting together is another familiar pattern of life for those of us who live in the shadows of life, away from mainstream participation in dominant cultural ideology. The crazy quilt symbolizes how we participate in life. It contains s variety of colors and textures within its borders with some of the pieces large and some odd-shaped, some old and some new, but all fitting together perfectly. There is no set pattern, color texture or design. Any piece of material gets sewn in wherever it will fit until there is a complete quilt.

The quilts made by women of color always bring memories to mind that are shared in Quilt University. The touch or sight of certain materials in a quilt tugs at our inner emotions which were created out of many different experiences and environments. The quilts that are made are a symbol of our lives. They can be bright and colorful, representing young love and everyday activities that bind us together. When we finish our work, the quilts will be a product of warmth, harmony, comfort and love, stirring many memories of our special friends and children. The art of quilting will be treasured and the memories that we share will last a lifetime.

Our life histories have missing pieces and can only be found by constructing all the craziness into a pattern in an attempt to find the missing pieces. As you will read in what follows, Harriet Powers provided a place for me to begin the search for pieces. Renee Walton provided a way to look at how to connect to the past. Alice Walker provided a way to stitch some of the pieces together to write books. Zora Neale Hurston provided me with the insight that quilting is not the only way to look for missing pieces. One cannot create an overall coherent pattern if the scraps are not available to connect the pieces of fabric or if the words are not available to write the text.

The crazy quilt is the only quilt found that does not need a pattern. Everyone brought a piece of fabric and it got stitched any place in the quilt. It's amazing that it turned out to be a completed quilt and everyone was able to identify their piece of fabric in the quilt. This represents the world African American women live in . . . one crazy event after another. Yet, they are able to stitch something good and beautiful in Quilt University.

PIECE 6

Patchwork Quilt

The learning that takes place in Academic University is best represented by the patchwork quilt. In making the patchwork quilt, the quilter who owns the quilt starts out with a pattern—"Jacob's Ladder," "Log Cabin," "Underground Railroad"—that determines the color and pattern of the fabric, and the size and shape of the pieces that will be needed. This individual buys or acquires all the fabric needed; the other quilters come only to help quilt, not to bring pieces to be quilted in. The pattern is worked on systematically, with each piece added because it fits into the overall pattern. When the quilt is completed, there are no surprises: the pattern is complete as intended. This is similar to the written curriculum of Academic University as it is laid out in a syllabus: The instructor lays out the pattern (the curriculum, including the syllabus and the sequence of lessons, assignments, and tests) and selects the fabric (the written texts to be read). The students are involved in the piecing together (that is, they write about others' published writings), but they do not bring their own "scraps" of knowledge to be worked into the overall curriculum.

The patchwork quilt appears to the uninitiated observer as a collection of bits and pieces of scraps of material—the kind depends on the era—calico, muslin, linen, silk or cotton. There is also a representation of class in the fabrics of the patchwork quilt. Silk represents the upper class, and calico, the peasant or lower class. Elaine Showalter notes that "the patchwork quilt has come to replace the melting pot as the central metaphor of American cultural identity. It transcended the stigma of its sources in women's culture and has been remade as a universal sign of American identity" (1989, p. 169). Yet, the patchwork quilt serves as a very powerful symbol of representation of the history of the lives, memories and treasurers of the African-American women who got little or no representation in the written text. Stitched in these quilt texts are valuable stories that can tell us much about the lives of African-American women. They can be triggered by reading the quilt text and telling the stories from an oral history context. This has caught the attention of contemporary scholars who are doing extensive research and writing on quilt culture. While quilting is the dominant world of women, men have captured the economic value of these material objects and are making a profit collecting and selling them. For African-American women the quilt is a symbol of an institution of self. It is the one artifact of aesthetic beauty that holds them together as a group and culture.

In researching the written texts about quilts and listening to the quilters tell their stories about quilts and quilting, I hear the deeply felt meaning of the African-American women, which can only be accessed by the women from a memory of time, place, and community of learners as outside participants of the dominant culture. There is not a thread to stitch together the two cultures to get one representation of two different theories outside African-American women and inside Euro-American women. No matter who we are, we all want to wrap ourselves in a quilt, speaking metaphorically, which gives us a warm feeling that makes us feel good about ourselves. This is evidenced by the comradeship I experienced when talking to African American women about their experiences with quilts—whether she received a quilt as a gift from a family member or friend, or she is a maker of quilts. I have heard them say such things as: *I have some quilts Aunt Nancy gave me years ago. I keep them in a cedar chest and when I want to remember something or get a sense of feeling I had of my family, I take them from the chest, put them on my couch, and sit on them; put them on my bed and cover my body with them and experience pleasant remembrances of the past by discovering a piece of fabric in the quilt that my aunt wore when she baked cookies in her kitchen with me beside her. I remember standing around the quilt frames when the women in the community got together to piece the quilts and share the experience of daily events about family, friends, community and church.* Great remembrances!

Patchwork Quilt
By Nancy Evans and Allie Grace, Evergreen, Alabama, 1958
Pieced Diagonal Block Quilt. Green and pink cotton fabric in diagonal block pattern. Machine sewn and tied with yarn.

PIECE 7

Home and School

I grew up in Evergreen, Alabama. Evergreen is in the southern part of Alabama, between Mobile, which used to be the state capitol, and Montgomery. If you want a time marker, I was in third grade when Pearl Harbor was bombed.

At that time, most of the people around Evergreen were farmers, including my grandfather. My grandfather, my mother, my sister and brother, and myself all lived together in Grandfather's house. Living there all together was wonderful. My grandfather was a sweetheart: my father had gone off and left us and he saw that we were taken care of. His house was a big old frame house, not a log cabin like most other farmers' houses. Our house's rooms had tall ceilings to accommodate all of Grandfather's antique furniture. The windows were wooden with latches—no screens. Of course, we had a fly swatter.

It was six steps up to the porch, and around the porch on each side there were wooden railings, to keep the kids from falling off. I would give anything to have a picture of that house. On the porch was a swing and some rocking chairs, all handmade. Through the front door was a hallway that cut through the middle of the house, with rooms on each side. In the hallway was a washstand with a pitcher of water in a bowl, so you could wash your hands.

Past the washstand on the right was Grandfather's bedroom, with a fireplace and wooden chairs around it. We all could sit there and listen to his stories. There was another bedroom, adjoining Grandfather's room—no one slept in there because we all wanted to sleep with my mother. On the left side of the hall was another big bedroom with two beds in it. My mother, my sister, my brother and I slept in that room—my brother was smallest, so he slept with my mother.

After that bedroom was another room—I don't know what we called it back then, but it was where we ate, the dining room. This room had a long wooden table with chairs on each side and each end. That's where we ate, and when company came, that's where we served the guests. Also in this room was a safe: a wooden cabinet that had two doors that were tin with a design that had been punched into them with a nail. It had a drawer for silver, and in it were beautiful china dishes.

Out of the dining room and down four steps was the kitchen—it was almost like an attachment but it was part of the house. That's where we did the cooking. We had an iron stove that burned wood. The chimney went out the ceiling to take the smoke out. There was an ice box in there. We took turns getting up and lighting the stove, to let it heat, and also going out to the well to bring the water in and putting it in a tank on the stove to heat. The one who forgot to bring the water in got in trouble the next day. We had a shelf where we set the buckets, sometimes two or three buckets. And gourds were hanging up on the rack, and that's what we drank the water out of. Going out the kitchen door, you would step onto a small square porch. Going down the steps to the right, you went into the garden.

Our school was named China School, and the schoolhouse was constructed by the men in the community who went into the woods and sawed down pine trees. They got hammer and nails, which they bought themselves, and built these little schools. They weren't connected with the Board of Education, like the white schools were, and they didn't get any funding except for some hand-me-down, outdated books. This was China School, located three miles from my Grandfather's house and holding kindergarten through eighth grade. It got its name from the chinaberry tree: In Evergreen there are a lot of chinaberry trees.

China School had one room, with the classes divided by red and white checked curtains—of the same oilcloth fabric they used to make table cloths. Back further was the lunch room, and those were the only two rooms we had. We had two outhouses: one for boys and one for girls. To get to the playground, we had to walk back a distance through the woods. There, kids would play basketball and run races around the track, which was a dirt path. We would also play horse shoes, Kick the Can, jump rope, and "Sally Walker," a game where you all join hands and go in the circle. One child sat in the center while the rest marched around singing,

> Little Sally Walker,
> Sitting in the saucer,
> Weeping and a crying
> For a cool glass of water.
> Rise Sally Rise!
> Wipe your weeping eyes.
> And put your hands on your hips
> And let your backbone slip.
> Shake it to the East,
> And shake it to the West.
> Shake it to the pretty one you love the best.

The one in the middle would choose "the one they loved the best" by facing that person and shaking, then tapping their hand. The line stopped while the one went out and the other went in. We would keep playing until everyone had a chance to go in that saucer. We played tag, too.

Our school transportation was walking. You had to walk the red clay, dirt roads for three miles, each way. We got our exercise. Walking those three miles, you were in tune with nature, because there were the trees, and the rabbits, and the squirrels, and snakes—oh, I hate those snakes. We had to climb over fences, depending on which way we went. If you went out the front door of Grandfather's house and crossed the road, across the road was the family cemetery my Grandfather owned. We walked alongside it then climbed over a fence with a barbed wire across the top, and cut through the woods —a long way through those woods, about a mile. When we got through the woods, we climbed over another fence and were at the Grace Mission Baptist Church. My Grandfather owned that church and the cemetery around it as well. From here, we turned down the main road and walked on another two miles to China School.

Alternatively, we could go out Grandfather's front door and turn left, down the road instead of through the cemetery. Down this road, we passed the White school house. It was about fifty feet from the house where we lived, a pretty, big, white-painted school with yellow school buses. Beyond it, we could get on that main road, turning right and walking on to China School. But this was not as safe, because when the White children would come up in the big yellow school buses after a rain, when there were mud puddles standing in the road, and we would meet the buses , the driver would try to catch us at one of those mud puddles to splash us. We ran to keep from getting that mud on us. And the White kids yelled names and laughed.

We studied reading, writing, arithmetic, history, literature—oh, I loved that. We read poetry, like "Trees" by Joyce Kilmer, *Beowulf,* and poems by Robert Frost. We read about Thoreau's experiences at Walden Pond. And a powerful poem:

> Let me live in my house by the side of the road
> Where the race of men go by;
> They are good, they are bad, they are weak,
> They are strong,
> Wise, foolish - so am I.
> Then why should I sit in the scorner's seat

Or hurl the cynic's ban? –
Let me live in my house by the side of the road
And be a friend to man.[1]

We had physical education classes, and some of the teachers did folk dancing: Irish and Scottish. They called it "exercise."

School at China School did not meet for as many months as the white school did because we had to help with the labor on the farm. We started planting in the Spring, in March and April. We planted corn, cotton, soy beans, sugarcane, and sweet potatoes. Mind you, the farmers—the men in the community—had already done all the cultivating of the land, getting it ready for the plants. They plowed the fields, opening up rows for the seeds to be planted. It was our job to drop the seeds in the cultivated rows—cotton seeds, corn seeds, soy bean seeds. Don't forget the watermelons: we planted them, too. The sugar cane was just cut down with a sharp knife and piled up; it came up each year without planting. The sweet potatoes were planted as well. In August, September, and part of October we were picking cotton and gathering corn and other vegetables. We also picked fruit from the trees—pear trees, peach trees, mulberry and huckleberry trees, and persimmon trees. And don't forget the blackberry patches: my Grandfather had a patch as big as this house, and all that was in there was those big juicy blackberries—and the snakes.

---

[1] By Sam Walter Foss, a New England poet and librarian, born in 1858.

We were in school after everything had been gathered: we started in October, and attended on through February, when the planting would begin again.

**Crazy Blocked Quilt
By Nancy Evans, Evergreen Alabama, 1930s**
Cotton fabric, crazy quilt blocks, pieced into rows in alternating diagonal block pattern. Two borders of strip quilting. Hand sewn, hand quilted, cotton batting.

PIECE 8

My Grandfather

I am at this place in my life, reflecting back on the learning I have experienced thus far, because my grandfather instilled in me to get an education so I could have a chance to have a better life and make more choices.

I didn't know what that meant. We were living in an environment that did not give an equal chance to be exposed to book learning and libraries.

I have always been inspired by the stories my grandfather told, and they have been in my memory all of my life. I did not know what "education" was, but I knew it was important and it was out there somewhere, and that someday I would find it. Once I started on my journey to find education, I never stopped.

I had a breakthrough by creating a "quilt university" to find a way to be successful in the academic university. To think that books of knowledge had always been there! Finding that knowledge in academic university has made a difference in the way I participate in life. All of this has been good. I found a voice, an identity. It has all been good. The journey has been long and worth it.

PIECE 9

Experience and Education

It is my belief that we must look backward in order to look forward, and must remember the past in order to know the future and be able to participate in the present. By accepting this, I can transform to another dimension of awareness from that in which I already exist.

Attending my mother's funeral a few years ago gave me a sense of self that I thought I had forgotten. I yearned to own one of the quilts that she stitched with her own hand, and to touch and see the materials she used to piece her quilts. This started a process of remembering that is overwhelming. I am attempting to find a way to describe the good feelings and memories that took place years ago—for me, and for everyone present—when the quilts were being made. This gives a sense of self that was forgotten, and a freedom in the form of recovering a lost past, which was not lost after all, but existed in the memory of the individual experience.

You only know a thing if you have experienced it. For example, a boat trip is an abstract idea until you buy a ticket, get on the boat and experience the ride. Then it becomes a learning experience. The quilt as a metaphor is an educational experience for African American women because it is a way to participate in self (personal). It includes self, family, and community involving self in everyday life experience. It creates a place and space where one can return in memory again and again to recreate self and relive history and real life experience.

In contrast, the school trains African Americans in the ideology developed by the dominant culture, and sends us back into the communities as missionaries of oppression and control. People of color have been trained to be carriers and consumers of the systems created to control us. The conditions of today have been determined by what has taken place in the past in the context of our experiences. Participatory learning is limited for black people because we are limited as to political, economic, and educational systems. This keeps us on the outside of a society that controls us through language packaged to keep us in place. What we don't have is a well-defined notion of what that place is, but still we must find a way to enter or connect.

Quilt University was a place where we did learn and were geniuses at playing the roles assigned. Quilt University gave us real educations, in the sense that "real education means to inspire people to live more abundantly, to learn to begin with life as they find it and make it better" (Woodson, 1990, p. 29).

Harriet Powers using her slave experiences to construct her story of survival through her quilt is an example of creating self wherever you are. Harriet Powers gave herself a real education. She stitched her thoughts in fabric where she could go back and read the quilt and have a sense of self and a connection of time and place. Her contribution has helped academic quilt scholars who used her work to create written text.

Dominant culture institutions of learning rely on products: book learning and written documents, both as sources of knowledge and as ways of recording students' progress. The people in positions of institutional power get to choose the language that is acceptable in the institutions. They get to assign the labels to products and bestow names (e.g., memory versus history), and to control the processing of products (e.g., scholarship and students), thereby "keeping the gate"—shutting out those who are historically outsiders to institutional culture. This is highly ironic in that insiders to institutions are the ones who in the first place created the labels that made others outsiders. They labeled others as "savages" in need of saving, and as products, objects, and tools whose existence is based in usefulness to others. Here, the salient metaphors for the dominant culture are the Library and the File Cabinet. The university of this dominant culture is Academic University.

Those who have historically been shut out of dominant culture institutions to one degree or another—people of color, speakers of languages other than English, homosexuals, people with disabilities, females and old folks—have often relied on processes and ephemeral products as their sources of knowledge. Labeled as inferior and un-authoritative by dominant culture institutions, these "outsiders" have always developed their own institutions in which their own criteria for what counts as knowledge have been paramount. Here, I am talking about one such institution, Quilt University. Quilt University relies on process, call-and-response, oral traditions and oral theories. People in them are experts at recognizing value in and making use of what others might throw away as scraps and in what others have to say. In Quilt University, "scraps" of knowledge and history get stitched together into quilts with coherent design and shared meaning. These scraps consist both of pieces of fabric that index particular historical events that are significant at the personal, local, and national level and that are stitched into the quilt, and of snatches of conversation—history, philosophy, economics, psychology, human relations, advice—that constitute valued knowledge and that are shared as the quilt is stitched. The metaphors here are Patchwork Quilt, Crazy Quilt, Scrap Bag, and Memory Bank.

PIECE 10

Cut Off from Book Knowledge

In my segregated school experience books were scarce: they were presented at the beginning of the school year, collected at the end of the school year, and stored for the next term. The "whites only" library housed many books that were not available to me. The playgrounds, restaurants, and the school bus service were off limits to the African American children living in the South with signs posted "whites only." We were only allowed to use facilities posted "colored only."

However, the family, community, school and churches were a haven that nurtured every African American person in the village. We were taught from an oral history handed down by our ancestors who brought the histories with them when they came over on the slave ships. When we sat around the fireside at night listening to the many stories my grandfather told, that kept us happy: we felt a sense of community where everyone looked out for and took care of each other. If one person in the community was in need, everyone went to his or her aid by supplying the need s of that person. The one-room schoolhouse was a place of nurturing because all the teachers were a part of the community and supported every member in the community. We had little or no discipline problems, and values and morals were reinforced each day. If a child got out of line, that child had to come before the school and family members where each one reinforced the other.

Grandfather told me to never let anyone or anything get between me and a good education (1) because I would have more choices in life, and (2) because then whites could not take our land. He acquired fifty acres sometime in the 1800s and was secure in the community because he owned not only the land but also Grace Mission Baptist Church and the family cemetery. He was the only colored person in the community allowed to vote because he paid poll taxes. His Cherokee Indian background caused him to have some fears about losing the land. He stated specifically, "Go to law school in order to know your rights; that way they will not be able to take the land." When I was young, I did not know what this meant nor how it could happen, but I knew it was important and I would find a way to get an education.

For eight years I walked the six miles each day to the one-room school house with a burning desire to get an education. During these walks I developed some very good critical thinking skills. I recited and memorized poetry while walking to school. I studied hard and was always at the top of my class. At the same time the teachers supported me and let me know they believed that I could do whatever I believed I could do.

Roles in the segregated community were very well defined: (1) you could not attend the big white school house that was fifty feet away from the Grace farm, and (2) you could not ride the yellow school bus that brought the white children to school. You could not enter the establishments that did not have "colored only" signs. This did not matter too much because Grandfather had another agenda; he created a home environment that nurtured me. The stories told around the fireside were powerful and have been able to sustain me throughout my life.

Life in two cultures and learning from two social contexts has been very complex and challenging in a segregated environment—specifically in an institution of higher learning, more so because the institution was not about me. Three cultures –white and black in the South and integrated in the North—each requiring a different socialization and I have experienced them all. Segregation had the most meaning because the parameters were well defined: you knew what you could and could not do. Not so for me in the integrated North where the issues of segregation were not out in the open.

Crazy Block Quilt, Detail
By Nancy Evans, Evergreen Alabama, 1930s
Cotton fabric, hand quilted.

PIECE 11

Entering Academic University

Arriving at an integrated institution of higher learning, Academic University was a culture shock to say the least. The institution was very much different from the segregated school I attended, and there was so much reading and writing about all kinds of unfamiliar subjects: Different cultures were included in the curriculum but very little about African Americans. This seemed to be segregation in a different way: Exclusion while claiming inclusion.

Through my early socialization I learned that people are different because of the things they have been exposed to while present in some very complex learning experiences. I have been able to understand how diversity gets played out in race, class and gender situations. The problems and issues in the North have been more complex than they were in the segregated environment because in the South we did not hear words like race, class, gender, and poverty. We had Jim Crow segregation, and at the same time our environment was well defined and enforced, so we knew our place and we used what we had to survive. There was an honesty about how white people felt about you. It didn't bother us because we had loving, caring families and communities to live in supported by the school and church which were our Institutions, and they served us well.

Growing up in a rural Southern community, attending segregated schools, riding on the back of the bus, not being able to attend the public libraries left little choice about what one could learn. The only thing I could control was my attitude about the situation. Not having access to written material had created an environment where learning came from an oral tradition. The stories told by the family members and the people in the community gave some good background for learning but did not prepare me for the written material I was exposed to in Academic University and had no background knowledge of. I understood the material but had difficulty writing it and not enough time to learn and keep up with the pace. At home in the South, we could learn anything we wanted to as long as we did not cross the color line that would definitely cause conflict. But in this environment I needed a different set of survival skills based on academic standards.

When I came to the North, I still recalled how during our fireside storytelling sessions Grandpa, who was the head of the household, always managed to say, "Go to school, get an education so you can have choices in life." At three years old, I had not known what he meant, but it sounded like something special because of the attitude and enthusiasm with which it was presented. This idea had taken root and has been in my memory all my life. I had not known what it meant nor had there been a means available to expand a knowledge base, but I had always known I would someday reach that place wherever it was.

It was this search that brought me to Academic University. I had finished the segregated high school as salutatory of my class. I had left Alabama on the L and M Railroad train to Nashville, Tennessee, and had earned a degree in business. After that I had come to Toledo, Ohio, searching for a job, because I had relatives here to look out for me until I was successful. My education had been put on the back burner when I got married and raised a family while being employed. I was able to help my children pursue their educations and at the same time learned how to interact with teachers in an integrated school setting. I was very successful in this area because I applied the skills I learned in my childhood environment: I called teachers to let them know that I was available for any problems and help they needed to support the school. Further, I arranged parent/teacher conferences to become acquainted with them. They always knew that I was as near as the telephone and would come if they needed me. The children were well aware of this and knew what we expected of them. We were a team and everyone had to do their part. This reminded me of my childhood experiences defined by the community.

Returning to an academic learning environment after being away for many years created some very challenging moments for me. The curriculum, courses, and language were new and I had no previous background in the subjects studied. This was a fact and challenge for me as well as the instructors because they had no knowledge of my background. Time was an important issue. I needed it to become familiar with subjects, learn and interpret the language, and apply concepts in a way that was academic as well as give meaning to my real life experiences. I needed more time.

Furthermore, thinking about the many experiences I had in the world before entering the academy and noticing how fragmented and unstructured they had been triggered a search for the missing pieces. I began to think critically about what I needed to do to participate in the scholarly learning environment where books and writing were the key. I began comparing and making sense of the structured experience in the academy where instructions were spelled out in writing. This was much different from my previous educational experiences where most of the material was presented orally.

I became a nontraditional student in an academy of traditional students who had background in the subjects studied and who did not have to deal with the world of work and school. I attempted to apply myself as a newcomer to the academy and expound some of the ideas that I had learned from anthropologists Jean Lave and Etienne Wenger's (1991) *Situated Learning*. In this required text for my masters-level Anthropology and Education class, Lave and Wenger presented a theory of inside/outside participation in a community of learning. They explained:

> By definition a newcomer is a person [the student] who enters a community of practice [the academy], and having little knowledge or experience in that environment must practice in a legitimate peripheral participation process with an old-timer [the instructor], who has mastered the academic process. Newcomers bring a new body of knowledge to the process. . . . Legitimate peripheral participation [provides] a way to speak about the relations between newcomers, old-timers, activities, identities, artifacts and communities of knowledge and practice. Legitimate peripheral participation concerns the process by which newcomers become a part of a community of practice such as in academia. (p. 20)

In the institution of higher learning, Academic University, I was a newcomer and I felt consciously, for the first time, the condition of being shut out of an opportunity to learn. As a child, going to segregated schools had felt all right—normal. But here I was, in the supposedly integrated North in the supposedly post-racism 1990s feeling shut out, unwelcome. I felt invisible and not included because I did not see the curriculums as being inclusive and representing all people on an equal basis. The language used was the most difficult part of the institution for me. I looked at what had—been written, what was being said, who said it and who was being let in to participate from an inside perspective. The academic institutions in the North were not shutting me out deliberately but in using what was easily available to them, they were shutting me out.

But at the same time, I was reading material—particularly the theoretical material—that not only invited me in but also explained why I felt shut out. More important, it was giving me ways of thinking that could allow me to help build places of learning where I and people like me could feel legitimate and included. Lave and Wenger described and analyzed how people learn to be part of a culture or part of a profession through "legitimate peripheral participation," whereby they had roles on the edges of activity—roles that were necessary and appreciated, but that could be done with limited knowledge and skill while the participant increasingly developed his/her knowledge and skill. The "apprenticeships" they discussed included people learning to butcher in a butcher's school as well as people learning to be non-drinking alcoholics in an Alcoholics Anonymous meeting. One example that appealed to me was learning to be a seamstress: the novice is given their first job of sewing on buttons. If it isn't done skillfully, they can cut the threads and do it again, no harm done. The novice would never be given the job of cutting out the garment, because if they made a mistake there, all would be wasted and the loss would be expensive. While their language was unfamiliar, at least Lave and Wenger's theory brought to mind that I was an outsider and the academy had an insider perception of community of learning. I needed to find a way to participate.

Being a participant in the academy of learners, grounded in practical experience and bringing a knowledge base of experience in the world instead of a written background of academic book knowledge, created a complex learning environment for me. I was a situated learner (1) attempting to transfer knowledge as experience in the academy, and (2) connecting with language in the academy to create new meaning. In the process, I discovered that my *self* was missing and I needed to re-create the past in order to get a sense of self. To do this, I needed to find some mentors or role models with experiences similar to mine, and then mirror these individuals to find the missing pieces in my learning experiences. The mentors I chose were quilters and those who have written from and about quilt culture. As it turned out, this would help me to find a way to be connected to the book knowledge in the academy.

Crazy Quilt, Detail
By Nancy Evans and Allie Grace, Evergreen Alabama, 1930s

PIECE 12

Quilting Frames and Theoretical Frames

A quilting frame provides a tool for handling the large amounts of fabric and batting involved in stitching a quilt. It allows quiltmakers to better handle the stitching, reaching as far across the material as their arms will go, and then rolling the material up on the frame to allow them to reach farther. The frame provides the necessary tension and focus for the quilter to manage lots of material and to bring definition to the design.

Growing up, I remember sleeping under quilt frames with unfinished quilts rolled on them, that had been raised by a simple pully to the ceiling of our bedroom—so we would have room to sleep. The men made the quilt frames out of four, two-by-two pieces of wood. Two of the pieces were about twelve feet long. When the quilt top was ready to be quilted, the long edges of the quilt were attached to these twelve-foot boards using pegs that went into holes bored on the end of each piece. When the quilting process started, the quilt top was stretched out flat on this frame, and the women sat along each side and stitched. As their stitching progressed, the quilt was rolled up onto the frame pieces, along each side, so the stitching could continue. The women quilting on each side came closer and closer as the quilting progressed. When the quilting was complete, the quilt was rolled clear up on these pieces. Then the pegs were taken out, and the completed quilt was taken off the frame. The frame was not part of the quilt, but the frame was essential to give access and shape to the quilting. It was the only way they could stitch it because they couldn't just hold the fabric on their laps.

Academic University has its frames, too. In academics, we are constantly referencing our theoretical frameworks. A theory is never true or false; it is simply useful or not useful. As I mentioned in the last piece, I found Lave and Wenger's (1991) theory of "legitimate peripheral participation" to be extremely useful. In Academic University, a theory is used as a tool and a frame to search for and focus on different data, usually written, that is useful to understanding a problem or making an argument. Like a quilt frame, a theoretical frame allows a researcher to access and bring order to lots of diverse materials and subjects. You take what you want, what fits in your frame, and leave the rest. (But as we will see later, quilters never leave the rest—scraps are material for another crazy quilt.)

In my experience there have been two key learning environments: one is inside the established academic learning process, and the other is experienced in everyday life. There is a place for both environments. The theory I set forth here is intended to bring focus and shape to how someone, like myself, who had had limited or no access to academic learning environments can enter into Academic University and be successful. Such a student needs to recognize that he or she must simultaneously participate in two learning environments: Academic University and Quilt University is. (It is helpful if a student's teachers recognize their two learning environments as well, but it is likely that the teachers will not be aware of a student's quilt university. It must be the responsibility of the student to hold fast to his or her quilt university and educate the teachers about it, at the same time that they are learning about academic university from the teachers.) It made sense for me to "quilt" my way through Academic University, learning the correct words to use and the correct ways to use them—correct, that is, for Academic University. But in doing so, I could not discard my materials, my words, and my skills from Quilt University: I had to use my learning and framework from Quilt University to make sense of and sew together my academic experience. It's a sort of double-speak, or code switching, in which we try to integrate two different learning environments: I speak it from oral tradition, what we see and what we experience. But when I write it with references to ideas and shapes from Academic University, then others can understand it, too.

The problem with current schooling practices is that the teachers, by and in large, have been in the academic learning environment for so long that they have no knowledge and no base of understanding the quilt environment that their students come from. Women's stories about quilts and quilting can give educators important insights into the lives of women and their learning environments consisting of street and community universities, throughout the world, where they stitch their thoughts, ideas, opinions, and assumptions in fabric. They stitch their journals in fabric. This may parallel educational theory, looking at theory as a road map where people guide their thoughts, opinions, and assumptions to guide research.

I had an experience the other day. I called up a lady whom I know as an educator. She was referred to me by a former student of hers, who told me that she makes the most beautiful quilts which she takes and displays at shows. I dialed her number. She answered the phone and recognized my voice. I told her the student had told me that she makes quilts. She got very excited that I wanted to talk about her quilts. She told me that she retired thirteen years ago. She told me that she taught herself to make quilts and had made one per year, with a total of thirteen. She had given one to each of her two children and her grandchildren. She told me that she wanted to tell me her story of how she got interested in making quilts. I call this "Aunt Niecy's Story."

Aunt Niecy was the lady that lived next door to the educator when the educator was a child in Georgia. Aunt Niecy did not have any children. She made the most beautiful quilts, and gave some of them to the educator, who still treasures them. The educator had gone to college, received her master's degree, and taught in the public schools. However, the quilt stories from Aunt Niecy were the most important experience in her life. She regrets that she does not have a picture of Aunt Niecy, but says she can see her face as vividly now as she did many years ago, and she is now deceased. I asked her had she thought about making a quilt and including a picture of Aunt Niecy in the fabric. I told her about the people I had seen on quilts that looked so real—Frederick Douglass and W.E.B. Dubois. She became very excited and told me that she was going to give this some thought.

Significant here is the fact that no matter where she went, to school and college, getting as much academic learning as she could get and giving it back through her own public school teaching, she counted her learning with Aunt Niecy and her quilts as her most important experience. It was a spiritual connection. When she had finished her academic teaching career, she taught herself to quilt as she remembered Aunt Niecy's having quilted. All she had to do was pull one of Aunt Niecy's quilts out of her chest, and it triggered her memory and her ability to learn to quilt herself. All the experiences were important and good, in academics and in quilting. But when it came right down to it, she returned to the quilting.

Crazy Quilt
By Nancy Evans and Allie Grace, Evergreen Alabama, 1930s
Cotton fabrics pieced without preset pattern into triangles then pieced together to create overall pattern. Hand sewn and hand quilted.

PIECE 13

Community in Quilt University and Lack of Community in Academic University

"Community" depends on the practice of regular communication between participants and potential participants in the community. Marian Schaprio (1994) reminded us in *Quilt Culture:*

> Quilt making was one of the most important female domestic activities for many centuries. In the collaborative, community-oriented art of the quilt, lap work gives way to an ambitious multi-layered work. Transcending the boundaries of class, race, country

of origin, and history, the quilt is a humanized, democratized art form. Even its subject matter – weddings, commemoration, friendship, freedom, political loyalties, and family records reflects rituals of community live.

My experiences in Academic University show a lack of the feeling of community which quilters and scholars have found is inherent in what I am calling Quilt University. Also in the book *Quilt Culture,* Hilliard (1994) noted:

> Most women's quilting, needlework and sewing went beyond both practical and aesthetic concerns: stitching became a habit of mind, a ritualized practice of connection making, unification, and harmonizing. This was missing for me in academia. Many quilts, especially the patchwork and crazy quilts are icons of a working community. Quilts offer complex visual solutions for deriving unity from diversity, they represent the enactment of coexistence , the value of differences acting together to shape a new whole, greater than the sum of its parts. A quilt is a map of devotion to doing and using as well as completion and the coexistence of these ways of seeing results in the narrative pleasure of an art. (p. 116)

Quilt culture is based on creating coherence and community from fragments and individuals. I take the following statement from Hilliard (1994) as supporting my argument for Quilt University as meaningful context for African-American women:

> The use of quilts as textual sites is also generously evident in much African- American quilting where complex visual forms were wedded to both Nsibidi symbology and to natural or cultural remnants. In some quilts Biblical narrative is retold in quilt form; in others, ancestral religious symbols are documented. African-American quilts often acted as historical, cultural, and religious maps directing from past to present. These quilts revived past cultural environments which emphasized religious symbols with meanings which could not always be put into words and thereby provided an immensely important instrument for teaching, for enlivening tradition and for providing protection in an otherwise hostile world. (p. 118)

Through quilts, African and African American women brought together diverse knowledge into coherent patterns, and expressed ideas and beliefs that were inexpressible in words.

Most important, quilts provided a vehicle for subverting dominant ideologies; quilted text enacted alternative readings of the world. Margot Kelley (1994) quoted educator Elsa Barkley Brown as saying, "The form of much African-American strip quilting is a conceptual metaphor for the world view of African-American women who typically create, a "polyrythmic," "nonsymmetrical," non-linear structure in which individual communities are not competing entities" (Kelley, 1994, 49). Not only are the quilts "conceptual metaphors," but they are also modes of communication. Hilliard (1994) noted:

> Quilts have a rhetorical purpose in providing a public space for naming and renaming the world. Permitting a reality to be known, defined, and communicated through shared visual code. They meditate the position of private person and public world. In the nineteenth century, when most women were not only denied representative voice in politics, but were also largely unnamed in public records of ownership, friendship quilts provided a vital record of existence, acting as an instrument of census taking. (p. 118)

The quilt was a record not only of individuals' existence, but also of groups' existence essentially the enrollment records of Quilt University. Hillard (1994) quoted Linda Lipsett:

> Prior to 1850, only the names of 'heads of families' were listed on government census records. The friendship quilt worked to name a woman's society as it reclaimed community from the margins.... [I]n instances, friendship quilts are the only remaining

> records of the women whose names are inscribed on them? We can imagine that the power of signature as seal of promise, commitment, and authority — a power held by men — was transcribed onto friendship quilts as the sign of cooperation and accomplishment by women. The quilt acts as mediator between the individual and the social realm, as an embroidered or stamped name was brought to public consciousness. The quilt's intimate, yet public nature, makes it an especially appropriate space for nominal inscription. Upon a quilt, a woman's name marked a place of protective care as it represented a social identity. (p. 119)

Quilt University is thus based in cooperation and communication, and through the products of the University—the quilts—individuals are visually and visibly integrated into the community of practice.

Coherence and community seem much more problematic in Academic University. The central problem keeping me out of the academic setting was language. Language (written language) is and has been a problematic area of transformation from where I exist to a viable place In the academy. Deborah Cameron (1992) explained this as a systemic rather than an individualistic problem, noting:

> [There] is a rhetoric of silencing," "alienation," and "appropriation" that pervades writing. If language

is not authentic it can undermine our capacity to transform self and the world we live in. This gives insight into not being able to connect effectively in academic ideology. (p. 128)

In contrast, in Quilt University alienation and isolation did not exist because everyone was included in the process/dialogue and was adequately rewarded for participation. In the words of Adrienne Rich (1976):

When we become acutely, disturbingly aware of the language we are using and that is using us, we begin to grasp a material resource which women have never before collectively attempted to repossess... . [A]s long as our language is inadequate our vision remains formless, our thinking and feeling are still running in the old cycles, our process may be revolutionary but not transformative. (p. 101)

In Quilt University, language is "graspable." In my early experiences in Academic University, it was not. Until I could grasp the language of Academic University, I could not formulate my experiences and visions in ways that participants in Academic University could grasp.

Women's experiences have not gotten equal representation in the construction of language that has power within dominant culture institutions. How can women find whole authentic selves through a process of personal transformation? This is true of most women but specifically true of African-American women who are broken by language in how they get labeled and processed in society. This leads African-American women back to self and their experiences in the quilt culture to heal themselves from • their broken experiences in the dominant construction of meaning and reality created in the social construction of environment by piecing quilts and telling stories of their everyday experiences. Cameron (1992) argued:

> My contention that there is a prejudice for writing and against speech might seem counter-intuitive. No one can be unaware that speech precedes writing both for the individual and for the culture, that most linguistic events are spoken rather than written, that there are non-literate cultures in existence, and so on. Yet, in literate cultures we find many linguistic forms stigmatized for no better reason than that they would never appear on a printed page. (p. 216)

Patchwork Quilt with Pieced Border
By Nancy Evans and Allie Grace, Evergreen Alabama, 1940s
Varied shades of pink and blue cotton fabric in geometric pattern with border on two edges of quilt blocks in star and stripe patterns. Hand sewn and hand quilted.

PIECE 14

The Quilt Connection

I chose the topic of quilting in part because I was looking for an artifact that would have a worldwide connection. I wanted to work with an idea that would connect people through tradition to a community of learners sharing a common interest, across time and space.

One day I went to my linen closet looking for an item and found a quilt top made by my grandmother more than eighty years ago. I have not been able to figure out how that quilt top mysteriously got into my closet. However, it brought back fond memories of my grandmother and all the fun things that she did, and how she and the women in the community used to sit around the quilt frame for many hours at a time making the tiny little stitches to hold the quilt together. I remember it vividly because I am the one that got called on to thread the needles when they had run out of thread. I do not remember too much about the stories they told each other, but I do remember how much they laughed and enjoyed each other's company.

That did it. I went to the phone and called a cousin whom I had not spoken to for a long time. When she answered the phone, I immediately asked her did she know anything about the quilts. She told me that she had some quilts in her treasure chest that my grandmother had made for her. She further stated that when she got lonesome and felt a need to remember her family, she would take the quilts from her treasure chest and remember her family. This convinced me that there is a connection between people and their quilts.

The connection is not only between people but across time. The tradition of stitching layers of fabrics together for warmth—quilting—is believed to be so ancient that it may have preceded the written word. The British Museum owns a carved figure of a pharaoh of the Egyptian First Dynasty, 3400 BC. The figure is wearing a mantle or robe covered with a diamond pattern that suggests quilting. However, the earliest surviving example of actual quilted goods is a carpet in the Leningrad Department of the Academy of Science of the former USSR, dating from between 100 BC and 200 AD. It was found being used as a floor covering in a tomb in northern Mongolia. Surviving evidence indicates that quilting was already a highly developed kind of needlework before it was introduced in European countries during the crusades. It has been assumed that the function and popularity of quiltmaking began in rural England as a practical way of providing warmth. There are numerous listings of fine quilts in estate inventories of the wealthy and noble classes in England in early centuries, but no mention of quilts in the property inventories of the lower classes. During the eighteenth and nineteenth centuries, it was customary for a young woman to make a baker's dozen of quilts for her dower chest. The thirteenth quilt of this group was her masterpiece, designed to display her skill with a needle.

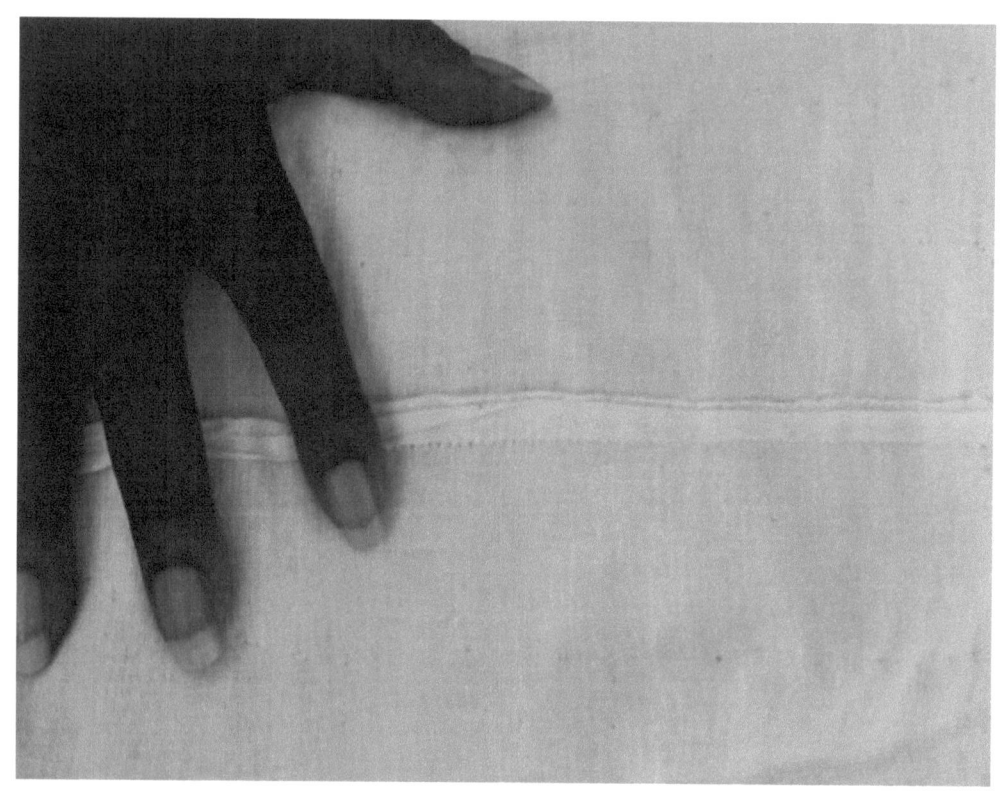

Quilt Back
By Nancy Evans, Evergreen, Alabama, 1938
Cotton, machine pieced and quilted.

PIECE 15

Call-And-Response in Quilt University and Academic University

Geneva Smitherman (1977) described call-response as an African-derived process which may be defined as follows:

> Spontaneous verbal and nonverbal interaction between speaker and listener in which all of the speaker's statements ("calls") are punctuated by expressions ("responses") from the listener. In traditional black churches call-response is often referred to as the congregation's way of "talking back" to the preacher....
> Like most other Africanisms in Black American life, call-response has been most carefully preserved in the church. It is a basic organizing principle of Black

American culture, for it enables traditional black folk to achieve the unified state of balance or harmony which Is fundamental to their traditional world view. Since that world view does not dichotomize life into sacred and secular realms, you can find call-response both in the church and on the street. (p. 104)

Smitherman (1977) gave the following example of call-and-response in the church:

Preacher ("caller"): My theme for today is Waiting on the Lord.
Congregation ("responders," all speaking simultaneously): Take yo' time, take yo' time. Fit it up, Reb! Preach it, Reb! (p. 108)

Smitherman (1997) quoted Jackson as explaining the significance of call-response:

The moral sanctity of . . . life [in African society] derived from the idea that all is spiritual and that the Supreme Power embodies the totality of the cosmos in one spiritual unity...the African continuum is essentially harmonious. Men, in building their societies, endeavor to reproduce this "divine or cosmic harmony." This is the basis of all ethical and moral behavior in the community life. (p. 108)

Quilt University is an apt place to use call-response because we have in this case a community of women who gather to affirm self and share with each other while quilting with fabric to make something good and beautiful. As they piece fabric and conversation together, the use their own language and methodology (call-response) to create new knowledge. Call-response could not be useful in isolation. In community, use of dialogue is important in forming a connection rather than being separate; this helps to validate the processing of knowledge.

Dialogue is significant in Quilt University because the call-response method would be invalid without a speaker and listener. Through dialogue with bell hooks, Patricia Hill Collins emphasized the importance of dialogue for creating meaning:

> For Black women, new knowledge claims are rarely worked out in isolation from other individuals and are usually developed through dialogues with other members of a community. A primary assumption... underlying the use of dialogue in assessing knowledge claim is that connectedness rather than separation is an essential component of the knowledge validation process. (p. 212)

Awareness of the call-response process has been most helpful for me to become clear about who I am and is one of the key *concepts* of what has been missing for me in Academic University. This has been helpful for me to accept my learning experience as being valid and necessary for survival as a person. I do not have to give up one culture to participate in another.

The difficult part was finding data to help me become aware of my African-American culture. My argument about not finding it in Academic University is valid. It is not there and may never be there because, for the most part, the university has no inside knowledge of what took place in Quilt University. There is no clue because they have not listened to a dialogue that is considered invalid (Black English). From my experience, the only way for Black stories to surface is for Blacks to tell and write about them in Quilt University, and then to bring them into Academic University.

In her analysis of Black English, June Jordan (1985) pointed to the significance of this dimension of an alterative epistemology:

> Our language is a system constructed by people constantly needing to insist that we exist. . . . Our language devolves from culture that abhors all abstraction, or anything tending to obscure or delete the fact of the human being who is here and now/ the touch of the person who is speaking or listening. Consequently, there is no passive voice construction possible in Black English. For example, you cannot say, "Black English is being eliminated." You must say, instead, "White people eliminating Black English." The assumption of the presence of life governs all of Black English...every sentence assumes the living and active participation of at least

two human beings, the speaker and the listener. (p. 129)

Survival skills are developed from the context of experiences. Built into Black English and Black culture is the spirit of resistance of a dominant institution that does not share experiences from the same context.

Alice Walker's writing process gave me a whole new way of looking at processes. She wrote from the confines of her culture, using everyday experiences within the context of Quilt University. It worked very well for her, even when her works were taken into Academic University. I am able to stay connected to the spirituality of her work, which is prevalent in the African culture from a world view context. This has given me a way to understand how I have been able to survive in a world that I did not understand. The missing pieces have been connected in a way so that I can process data from Quilt University and Academic University without assimilation.

How can the academic process accommodate two perceptions of different experiences? Through call-and-response, we can see how African Americans have had to live and function from two perceptions: their own and the dominant culture. This shapes the roles African-American women play in their daily lives.

Call-response methodology is used by African-American women to help them create a process to function inside of themselves and subjectively in a daily environment. In the past and in the present, their socialization has not allowed them to develop scientific theories because they did not know how. From a call-response context, by quilting pieces together African-American women were able to code meaning in a space created for survival. Where else can they begin to process except from the institution of self? They had and have no powerful institution to dictate rules and policies. Quilt University and the stories told there offer some possibilities.

PIECE 16

Missing Pieces/ Finding Pieces

I relate to women who have found in quilting a way to find themselves. Thoerist Donnel-Vogt described the quilt as "first of all a speculum by which a woman looks into herself, and when she finds her unknown and disregarded beauty, she can find the courage to prevail along with others for her share of the world" (in Elsley, 1994, p. 8). We each have to find our own beauty and know our own knowledge.

What was missing for me in Academic University was the recognition of my knowledge as authoritative, valuable and necessary. The problem stemmed from the fact that my knowledge was not written down where it could be read, analyzed, validated, and interpreted in a language that represented my basis of knowing. My knowledge was created in Quilt University where it was stitched in fabric representative of the people who learned in the quilt context while talking — telling stories by using an oral text. In this sense, members of the institution who were outsiders to this method of learning and had no way to connect to the language used, classified this method as invalid and not to be accepted in an institution of higher learning. What was I to do? I couldn't get educated in the sense that I couldn't write a thesis and get a degree because my method was "invalid." Framing up my contents in Quilt University, using the trappings and trim of academic university, was what I needed to do to be recognized as valid. The *contents* were valid; they needed a *form* that could be recognized within the institution.

Why was I not included in the institutional structure and design of the academy? The social context of my life was different from the traditional, authoritative environment established by the dominant culture. My cultural environment was not included in the established, traditional, authoritative, written curriculum presented in academic classrooms. Instead, the contextual source of my learning took place in segregated oral environments. My learning was processed in a university created by women who quilted and stitched their thoughts, ideas and experiences in fabric. They told stories about their lives as a visual symbol to be read by looking at the fabric and design and associating it to a person, place, or time. The stories were to be read orally because each piece of fabric triggered a memory of a past experience that became a piece of history not included in the conventional written history books. Not wanting to give up self to an unknown place in the university, I began looking at the bits and pieces which began to surface in a messed up learning experience.

The quilt came to mind as a place to look for meaning in life. Speaking of Alice Walker's use of quilts, Donnell-Vogt noted that "putting together the pieces of 'messed up curtains,' torn in a fight between two women, Celie and Shrug in *The Color Purple,* these women reconfigure their bond. Guilt is transformed into quilt as discarded fabric and the rejected women are sewn into something whole and beautiful" (in Elsley, 1994, p. 56). For many women the bits and pieces are made of time and words.

This kind of transformation could not take place in the university because of lack of words to write as meanings in a book and there is not a place for negotiation. Sewing is one way for women to begin the process of self-reclamation because it represents, more than other activities traditionally associated with women, a powerful and elemental symbol of connection. The background knowledge provided in classes did not provide me a way to connect to the written word and create meaning because it was a language that I did not know. The whole problem boiled down to one need: the need to find a way into the academy of formal education. I began by looking for some role models who had backgrounds and goals similar to mine. I needed to find women who had succeeded in completing the educational process in a university or otherwise had gained full admission to dominant cultural institutions. I wanted to reflect on their life histories as a way to connect past experiences with present and to see if and how their histories were significant in my life. In the process of looking for women with whom I shared a common bond, I found Harriet Powers, a slave quilter who had only her experience from which to create her history through quilting because she could not read or write. I found Alice Walker, a writer and quilter who had gone through the educational process and shared a common bond with Harriet Powers. I found Renee Walton, a local Toledo quilter who used the quilt as a way to stay connected to her past and ancestors. And I found Zora Neale Hurston, an anthropologist and folklorist, who proved that quilting can be done with words as well as fabric. I reflected on and analyzed the lives of these African-American women. I concentrated on the tools they used, including the quilt, and the part played in developing survival skills from a cultural context. What meaning did the quilt play in connecting history, heritage, culture and tradition? What significance did the quilt play in the lives of my mentors?

PIECE 17

Why Life Stories of Quilters?

The big issue was finding a way to connect the personal past and transform it to the present time. What impressed me about the lives of the women I have chosen to write about is that they learned to trust in their own inner strength as the only source upon which they could rely: since they could not fully trust the world they lived in, they learned to *trust* in their own intuition. The quilt nurtured them and kept them warm, while at the same time giving them space and a place to be with self, tell stories and write books.

Every cultural transformation begins with the individual. The individual voice important because other voices send women suggestions such as "be quiet," "be good," "be invisible," "you are too old," and "you are not intelligent enough." From a cultural context women should just drift and let things happen:

someone will come along and rescue you (not true). The inner voice as power can be seen from Harriet Powers's beautiful quilt and the story captures the spirit of the people who share in her story.

Alice Walker's inner voice suggests she writes books for others to read while stitching fabric accessing memories. Renee Walton listens from the inner voice of everyday experience in order to maintain a sense of self and stay connected to her past. Zora Neale Hurston left a legacy in her books about her people in their natural environment using vernacular language.

Women need to take care of self and share their work and lives with one another in order to form peer mentoring networks and to form a positive experience which is important in maintaining identify in our everyday lives. Both Powers and Walker shared their life experiences. This made them available for others to read and interpret. Walton stayed in touch by looking for way to connect the past with the present. Hurston was interested in writing folklore from the original storytellers in the community in which she grew up. I participated in the process of connecting with women who had similar experiences to my own. They lived in society and succeeded regardless of their circumstances in life. Through connecting with them, I worked to find a way through the conflicts of slavery as well as my personal past—to transform my personal past into my present two worlds of experience and academia.

The "change" process in life, which is constant, affects all aspects of the way we live in the world. Our habits, opinions, desires, pleasures, pains, and fears do not remain the same; new ones come into existence and old ones change. I am impressed by the way Powers, Walker, Walton and Hurston teamed to trust their inner strengths as the only source they know they could rely on. The quilt nurtured and kept them warm and at the same time gave them a place and space to be with self. By choosing individual life histories I realized that issues affecting the lives of women—and especially women of color—are systemic and not individual after all. If one does not live and work within the system, one can be crushed by the system. If women try to step outside the boundaries that men have created to keep them in place they are looked upon as trouble makers or radicals. But these four women stepped outside of the boundaries and didn't get crushed. Instead, they extended the boundaries.

Patchwork Quilt
By Nancy Evans and Allie Grace, Evergreen Alabama, 1940s
Varied shades of red and white cotton fabric in geometric pattern with solid white border. Hand sewn and hand quilted.

PIECE 18

Quilting History: Harriet Powers

I am inspired by Harriet Powers's desire to hold on to her life history through the quilt she created and in which she stitched her story for others to interpret. Harriet Powers, known for her Bible quilts, was a slave and then a freed slave. She lived and died in Athens, Georgia, from 1837 to 1911. Circumstances did not change Harriet Powers's determination to succeed regardless of having to sell her first and favorite Bible quilt—her "darling"—for five dollars in order to survive. Further, she wanted the story written down in order for it to be passed down for others to read, reflect on and experience.

According to Mary Lyons (1993), Powers could neither read nor write but she had a life story she wanted to tell and leave as a tradition for generations who came after her. The quilt is the vehicle she chose to tell her story. She made other quilts, but her Bible quilts would become a memory of her spiritual life. Powers has two known surviving quilts. One is owned by the Smithsonian Institute and the other by the Museum of Fine Arts in Boston.

Powers is recognized as creating history within a tradition of quilted history. Gladys Marie Fry (1990) stated in *Stitched From The Soul:*

> The quilts form a direct link to traditional tapestries made by the Fon People Abomey in the ancient capital of Dahomey, West Africa. Powers' quilt can be compared with Dahomean tapestries in design, construction, technique and the retention of the stories associated with pictorial representation. The design has been handed down for hundreds of *years,* often referred as "living history books." They vary in subject and design because the individual design suggests which stories relate to oral tradition and oral history and *which* stories relate to symbols. (p. 85)

Quilts have histories, and quilts *are* histories. Lyons (1993) described one of Powers's Bible quilts:

> The quilt is made of 299 appliquéd pieces of cloth. Each panel depicts a scene from the Bible. Twelve years after completing her first quilt Harriet Powers completed her second story-quilt, one that combines Biblical incidents with local folk tale. Her quilts are

> visual masterpieces of creative imagination and aesthetic expression. Her entire communication with the world was visual and oral, which she expressed in her mutative quilts, using themes from her own experiences and techniques.. Her love for stories from oral tradition consists of local legends, Biblical stories and astronomical occurrences. (p. 24)

Lyons (1993) detailed how conflicts of naturally occurring events in the stories stitched by Harriet Powers from her memory were not believed because she had no scientific theory to prove her points. For example, in an oral history of her quilt, Powers described one block as depicting "the dark day of May 19, 1780. The seven stars were seen 12.N. in the day. The cattle all went to bed, chickens to roost, and the trumpet was blown. The sun went off to a small spot and then to darkness" (Lyons, 1993, p. 26).

These words did not prove what happened. However, fireballs or meteors are relevant occurrences recorded in scientific literature for the year 1846: *The American Journal of Science and Arts* (May 1847) states that meteoric showers were visible on the evenings of August 10 and 11, 1846 (Freeman, 1996, p. 104). Quilt scholar Roland Freeman (1996) explained:

> The real significance of Harriet Powers' explanation of her quilt blocks is that oral history turns out to be startling accurate. This former slave depicted stories that she had only heard, never read,

and that paralleled paranormal scientific records. But times were changing in Harriet's day, and she knew intuitively that the quilts she had so carefully and lovingly created should be explained in written form for those who would examine them in later years. She did this with the help of someone who could write. She got the stories that had most impressed her recorded just as in the quilt itself where Harriet Powers expressed both her life experiences and her American heritage. (p.104)

Often when people see the Harriet Powers's Bible quilt they respond intuitively to her images and recognize that her quilt possesses incredible integrity and meaning even if they're neither versed In the Bible nor know African-American history. It is also powerful in its cross-cultured use of imagery with echoes of African culture. When you add the poignancy of her story, it is an almost overwhelming icon.

PIECE 19

Quilting As Connecting: Renee Walton

This is my interview with famed African-American storyteller, quilter, and quilt collector Renee Walton of Toledo, Ohio. I am putting this in the form of questions and answers, as it occurred in the interview: This entire piece is interview, so Renee Walton's words are italicized as one long quote.

Thelma: How long have you been quilting?
Renee: 'Been quilting since I was a girl.
Thelma: How did you get started?

Renee: Well, when I was a girl my momma used to get together with ladies. At the time I thought it was strange to see women coming from so many different places; bring their little scraps and their little baskets and they would have their little needles and their threads in their hands and there was this big thing they would set up in the room. It looked like a big table. Momma had a big table.

The only time you would see them getting together is when there was a birthday, a funeral, or if there is a wedding, or if someone had something happen bad that night with husbands. They would call a meeting and all of them would come together and they would talk about these things and what each one could do to help the one that was in trouble. But, the quilt kept them busy while they would talk.

That was the whole purpose of that quiltmaking and these ladies would be setting up in that room sometimes three to four hours just be talking about so and so's problem or the young girl who had a baby or the wedding that was last Sunday, something like that. They would quilt. It didn't matter what color anything was. It didn't matter that the stitching was not right on the quilt. The point of it was that they all came together at a time when somebody needed somebody's help. That's what it was all about and I was setting watching it as a child, thinking of how nice it must be. And as I got older, comig up, these quilts that were made, they were given away. They were given away to the homes of the ones who had the wedding or the baby or the problem or whatever else that went on that day. The quilt was made for that purpose.

And I remember one time hearing this lady, her name was Ms. Hamilton, and I remember her saying one time to my mother, she says, "Now are you sure that green is going to go good with that blue?" (ha, ha, ha). And my momma started laughing (ha, ha, ha) and she said, It don't none of it matter because we don't have all these colors in our house, do we? We are just going to make them, put them on your sofa, put them on your chair, put them on your bed, do whatever you want to do with those quilts. But each one was made with sooooooo much love in those quilts.

Today, I own a quilt that was my great grandmother's that she made herself. And one day my mother decided to set down and teach me some of those stitches. It took me a long time to learn how to do those stitches for those quilts. My momma said, "There is no need to rush." I had all the time in the world to learn how to make a quilt. So, eventually I came in as I got older. I was about ten or maybe eleven years old when I first came in on my first quilt to help make. And, I can still remember that quilt. The side that I did not look all that great (ha, ha, ha), but my momma (ha, ha, ha) said that was the most beautiful side of the whole quilt with that little piece I had made. And, as I got older I became very fascinated in quilt making.

The only kind of quilts that I will collect, even today I collected quilts, but the only kind I will collect is those made by Black women. And, I have to know something about the quilt before I buy them. If I don't know anything about the quilt I won't buy the quilt. You've got to give me some history about each quilt that I possess.

Thelma: Why do you want to buy the ones made by Black women?

Renee: Because that's who I am, I am a Black woman and I can connect only with what Black women's struggles were about. And, every time I see a quilt that's made by a Black woman I think about those women that sat around that table with my momma and I say to myself, What baby was born during this quiltmaking? Or, What wedding had taken place during this quiltmaking? You know what I am saying, What excitement went on through the day that this quilt these women had sat around and talked about while they were making it? I came across one quilt one time, I guess I had to have been about 30, and I came across this one quilt. It was one Black lady by herself that made this quilt and I asked her, "How did you make this quilt?" She said, "You know during the time I made this quilt I just lost my youngest daughter and this quilt made me feel that I was as close to my daughter as if she was still alive."

So, I remember what momma said. That it's the quiltmaking that brought it all together. Made you feel that you were close to something or close to somebody (ha, ha, ha). It's so funny how I think about that now because it's so funny because it's like I ain't never had no reason to forget none of it. Just remember it. When that lady said she had lost her daughter and because of that quilt kept her so close to her daughter that she had to keep making it until she finished it. I asked, "How did you feel?" She said, "I knew that my baby weren't dead. I knew then I would always have her as long as I could hold onto this quilt." The mother eventually passed away, but her other daughter remembered me coming, talking to her mother about the quilt.

And I eventually got the quilt. But as long as she was alive she kept that quilt. And, the daughter gave the quilt to me. She just gave me the quilt. She too was up in years and she said she knew with me, I would take care of that quilt. And to this day I still take care of that quilt. And I thank God for my mother, because my mother taught me to love quilts. My mother also taught me to love old people that carries all the knowledge. It is those old people, and through those quilts where the old people's hands touched to keep all the knowledge hidden inside. And, I ask those questions again. Why did you make that quilt? What was the reason? What were you thinking the day when you made this quilt?

So, now I'm in possession of a Slave Quilt. I have a Slave Quilt that I got and the quilt belonged to a slave woman. And the pieces are that of her husband's and two sons. I treasure that quilt. I treasure that quilt because it helps me to stay in touch with Africa. All those beautiful sisters that I will never know by name or by face but that I will know through their quilts. I will know them through their quilts.

PIECE 20

Quilting As Process: Alice Walker

Alice Walker, for me, became the ideal mentor for me because of the similarities in our background and concepts of spirituality. That came out of growing up in the south which molded her childhood and grounded it in the land and customs of parents, family and older residents of her community. Giving her the starting point for her narratives which are shaped by the rural life of Georgia where there were cotton fields, barbed wire fences, sharecroppers' shacks and red clay gullies. Although her work is fiction, I vividly remember the scenes she describes in her writing as real. Lillie Howard (1993) comments on how Walker's writing about the present is grounded in her historical sense of the past:

> Walker's understanding of the history and culture of the South informs her stories of survival with a way of seeing the contemporary world and a context for expressing the accumulated meaning of life. She believes that nothing is ever "a product of the immediate present." As a result, she uses Southern history — past and present — in order to achieve a wholeness in her fictional creations, a wholeness which she finds elusive in the private and public lives of her people. (quoted in Freeman, 1996, p. 149)

In an interview with Ronald Freeman (1996), Walker said:

> I think my whole program as a writer is to deal with history just so I know where I am . . . I can't move through time in any other way, since I have strong feels about history and the *need* to bring it along. One of the scary things is how much of the past, especially our past, gets forgotten. (Freeman, 1996 p. 153)

On the other hand, Walker is grounded in her sense of spirituality. Howard (1993) notes:

> Walker admitted she was "preoccupied with the spiritual survival, the survival whole of my people," but that her specific preoccupations lay with

> "exploring the oppressions, the insanities, the loyalties, and triumphs of black women. For me, black women are the most fascinating creations of the world. Next to them, I place the old people — male and female — who persist in their beauty in spite of everything." (quoted in Freeman, 1996, p. 149)

Alice Walker used quilt culture as a real base from which to write. That is a third reason she was the ideal mentor for me: Inspired by quilt texts, she pieced written, printed texts. Howard (1993) analyzes Walker's fiction:

> The quilt has been a center from which Alice Walker writes here books. The quilt motif that appears so frequently in *The Color Purple* is an apt metaphor of the network of human lives Alice Walker believes must and can eventually save us. Fit together over the years from pieces of clothing the family owned, symbolizing both continuity of generations and the fragmented past of the black race, the quilt is an artifact taken up in time of pain and suffering. It is, along with the unflinchingly honest letters Celle writes, her overture to the world. In a symbolic gesture Celle gives the quilt to Sofia when Sofia leaves her abusive husband, Harpo observed, their kinship in the pattern of the quilt. (quoted in Freeman, 1996, p. 150)

Walker never lost sight of this world; she looked not for an externally imposed God or religion but at a divinity arising from interaction with nature, community and self. I identify with Walker's concepts because she came through the system and developed writing skills from which she could create characters from the concept of Quilt University to move through time from the past to the present by writing books. This, she has done, by returning to the experiences she had in the Southern heritage.

PIECE 21

Zora Neale Hurston

Zora Neale Hurston, though she does not talk explicitly about quilts and quilting as Alice Walker does, still writes from Quilt University. Zora Neale Hurston was an anthropologist, novelist, folklorist, and creative force of the Harlem Renaissance. She was a gifted person with a vital spirit who had a great Influence on women of color who followed after her, including Alice Walker. Hurston left Academic University to return to her Quilt University—Eatonville, Florida—to collect and document the stories she had learned as a child. She pieced the collection called *Mules and Men* by "stitching" together stories that she had collected over five years using "threads" of dialogue. That is, the stories were separate pieces when she collected them, but she formed them into a whole by piecing them together, putting them into the context of people's conversations and experiences.

Hurston is my fourth mentor because she depended on herself, she resisted assimilation, and after having succeeded in

Academic University (receiving a Ph.D. in Anthropology from Columbia University), she returned to Quilt University. There she wrote in the vernacular, outside the university. But later, her works were brought back into Academic University where they are now canonized as great works.

Zora Neale Hurston's works celebrate the folkways of African American people in the rural South. Hurston spent a lifetime collecting stories, legends, myths, and songs of her people to prove that a different culture does exist among Black people and that this culture is as complex and as sophisticated as Anglo or European culture. Zora did not feel that she was a deficient human from an inferior race of people. She felt that her people should not focus on the problems but should recognize and reinforce the richness of Black life. Alice Walker said that the quality she felt is most characteristic of Zora's work is its "racial health: a sense of Black people as complete, complex, undiminished human beings" (Howard, 1993, p. 6).

The feeling of racial pride and well-being came naturally for Zora Neale Hurston because she grew up in the all Black town of Eatonville, Florida. Alice Walker noted that the city was not only populated by Blacks, it was also governed by Blacks. There were small businesses that the people of the town supported. Hurston's experience of the South was very different from that of many African-Americans of her time. Throughout her life she held onto what some considered an idealized view of the South and she was sharply criticized for it.

Zora was critical of the Civil Rights Movement, integration and desegregation. Her views came from a belief that Blacks and Whites should remain separate because she celebrated the rich tradition and culture of her own people. She felt that it would be lost through integration. For me this is similar to what I think about assimilation and academic ideology. Women of color should be able to embrace both worlds and be able to carve out a piece of both worlds for themselves In some way, according to need, interest, and desire. Peterson (1994) noted:

> The Black woman's very life depends on her being able to decipher the various sounds in the larger world, to hold in check the nightmare figures of terror, to fight for basic freedoms against the sadistic law enforcement agencies in her community, to resist the temptation to capitulate to the demands of the status quo, to find meaning in the most despotic circumstances and to create something where nothing was before. (p. 33)

Each woman Hurston created tried to carve a little piece of the world out for self in some way. What is interesting is how each woman grew in courage and confidence in self. Hurston, drawing from her own experiences, brought to life these women and the circumstances that shaped their lives.

The culture of resistance is an important aspect of socialization for people processed outside of a dominant culture. The experiences these people have while living outside a dominant culture are unique, varied and culture specific. Only the people who live in an outside culture know the reality of these environments. The difficult part of being in an outside culture is the survival techniques that have to be used to participate in the dominant culture which is in control, distributes the material resources and the educational processes. This creates a variety of experiences for outsiders, at the same time sends mixed messages about reality and identity to the outside culture.

When I wrote *Piecing a Thesis in Quilt University* as my master's thesis (1999), I looked at one group from an outside culture — African American women quilters because (1) I could identify with this group, as they are a part of my African American heritage; (2) I wanted to learn from natural data; and (3) I was a participant observer in this group. Zora Neale Hurston's work served as a model for me to collect and write these stories.

PIECE 22

Conclusion: Piecing Society

There are common threads that run through the whole universe. You've just got to piece it together.

If your body of knowledge is different from my body of knowledge, does that make your body authentic and mine inauthentic? Or, is it just different knowledge? How can I validate my way of knowing at the same time I accept yours? How can we share our differences in a way that will empower both of us to grow in the direction each of us chooses to go while sharing different knowledge and experiences?

If this sounds off-beat, I can assure that it is not. I am still thinking about stories and how they relate to life and the universe. Somehow I know that the stories people tell or do not tell help create the rules that construct society. At this time, I feel something is missing because of all the negative reactions going on in media stories, written stories, political stories, and legal stories—for instance, the witness in a trial is a storyteller. The lawyers and judges get to decide what story they want to use to determine what they want to do with the victim.

From taped interviews on oral history, all kinds of data come to mind which do not seem to be about what I want to write about, but somehow I believe they are. That's the crazy quilt. Through my work I ask, How can I use theories to link my data to other stories as a way to create patterns, to sew together the scraps and interpret the pieces of data I have collected? One thing is for sure: I have more questions than I have answers at this point.

The process of piecing a thesis gave me insight to personalizing life—getting in touch with what matters most in life (Osbourne, 1999). My thesis simply looked at our individual and collective selves. It showed how being in touch with self from the foundation or center is helpful in how we relate to the world we live in. My mentors then and now—Powers, Walton, Walker, and Hurston—and their work encouraged me, and encourage me, to keep going when I wanted to quit, and when I want to quit. My thesis journey was not all connected to Quilt University. Hurston gave me an outside perception of African American history in her writing in the original language the experience of our people. All four women gave me a way to connect to a past that I had not known about: my history, my culture, and my people. Grandpa had started the process by giving me some basic ideas in bits and pieces. I had to complete the crazy quilt of my thesis, and in completing it, I found what

CONCLUSION: PIECING SOCIETY

I needed to know to create a place from which to participate in the world in a self-defined context.

Piecing the thesis was a very valuable and rewarding experience—and re-piecing it a decade later has been another. When I first pieced these pieces into my thesis, I acquired self-fulfillment in the process by gaining a way to identify self, validate self, and accept spirituality that has been the guiding light on my journey to reclaiming a self which I thought I had lost. In the process I discovered I had not lost anything. Self was only *misplaced* because I did not have the information I needed to connect what I knew with what I needed to know in the two different learning environments—Quilt University and Academic University. I could only grasp bits and pieces in fleeting moments because I did not know how to write them down. However, I did take notice and was determined to find a way to connect some of this data.

While being attracted to quilts, their stories, and people, I have found that more and more bits and pieces of information came to mind, sometimes from unexpected sources. For example, one day I went to my doctor. In conversation with him I mentioned that I was interested in quilts. He started telling me about his experiences with quilts. He described the quilts his grandmother made and the warm feelings he got when he came in touch with these quilts. For another example, the person who typed my thesis in 1999 told me how refreshing it was to share with me my story because it revived her interest in quilting. She showed me some beautiful quilts she was making for her grandchildren. It is motivating to share the enthusiasm with people and see how they respond when I mention quilts. This helped me to know, early on, that quilts, their stories, and the people involved would be my area of concentration for research and study.

Initially, when I came to write my master's thesis, the problem for me was finding a way to do it. Quilt culture was not part of academic university; this left me needing to learn academic language. I attempted to do research in other, "more academic" areas of study, but the subjects caused me to shut down because I could not relate to the theories used and was not included in them. Once I got grounded in quilt culture, however, these other areas opened up to me because the quilt gave me a center to work from, thereby enabling me to participate in other areas of study.

There is something magical about piecing a quilt or piecing a book. The creative process takes over and pulls gentry toward a higher self-awareness, and the thought process is not so much about piecing a thesis or making a quilt, but more about constructing your own life.

Working with the hands is meditative work which provokes the thinking process and ideas form. Working with my hands—whether piecing a quilt or a book—keeps me in tune with self by being a reminder and connection to the past, and helps me to live in the present by continually restructuring my everyday life. Roland Freeman (1996) wrote:

> The world of quilting by African-Americans provides us a profound example of how from scraps barely enough for survival, we created beauty, and

CONCLUSION: PIECING SOCIETY

then engaged the knowledge and aesthetics we found around us, sharing what we knew and incorporating what we learned—simultaneously becoming part of the mainstream, and yet continuing our distinct expressive culture. Our quilting is our history, and as a quilter said to me, "It comes from our hearts and souls." (p. 379)

By quilting we become makers of our own history rather than consumers of others' history. Once you participate in a creative process—be it in Quilt University or Academic University—you become part of it. Quilting is about whether you are alive in the moment you have.

The data I assembled for my thesis, and reassembled in this book, have helped me to understand that Quilt University and Academic University are necessary realities in real life. The challenge for me was and is to learn to function effectively in both environments. I now understand that writing is a necessary tool for learning. Data need to be written down in order for the people who come after to get a sense of what took place in past history. Oral history is important because it has always preceded the written word. Harriet Powers could not read or write, but she found a way to tell her story that left a legacy for others to use in their experiences. Starting from a point in slavery was a very good place for me to start in this process. First of all, that is the beginning of life for most African Americans in this country. Starting with slavery gives a connection to the past. Harriet Powers's story and her quilts gave much insight into conditions that slave women had to live under. Powers's story was the foundation and beginning of the process in Quilt University for me. Her work has enabled me to uncover my past and enlarge my present by knowing the context of her contribution to the world.

Alice Walker accomplished storytelling through her writing. She has written many thing I wish I could have said. She believes that writing and speaking are inseparable. She has been successful in Academic University, but she returned to the quilt to get a sense of history and self, and to create characters to write her books. This has taught me that our history is buried in someone's memory and it needs to be discovered and written down.

There is a spiritual self that guides me to keys that help me get in touch with my true potentials. I am attracted to the quilt as my center to work from. In the process of writing my thesis, I gained confidence that I can reach the goals I set for myself, and I came to feel free to be who I am. That feeling has continued. It does not matter whether you lived in a log cabin or a palace: The process of learning is the same. The data used to write or speak is what makes the difference. I learned that once I validate self, others validate me. Before I got involved in quilt culture very few people talked to me. I do not know how the word got around that I am interested in quilting, but many people talk to me now, mostly about quilting. It has been like planting a seed and watching it grow. It seems like the wind scattered the seeds in many places. I now believe I can learn, define, process, and integrate a different language into an accepted social practice and participate in a way to meet the requirements of Academic

CONCLUSION: PIECING SOCIETY

University. I will never give up Quilt University because this is my center to work from and it matters to me.

Through the process of piecing a thesis then writing a book, I learned many things that will help me in staying centered in academic environments as well as in everyday experiences. I learned many new things in my research. I learned a new language which has enabled me to write. Further, I found that women had many texts that appeared to be lost. I am discovering that the data are not lost, but need to be written down for others to read. These writings may be an assignment in Academic University or a quilt in Quilt University. In Academic University the writing can be read from written text. In Quilt University the quilt can be read orally by looking at the scraps associated with a person, time, or place.

Academic University for me is a patchwork quilt where there is an outline of data to be followed to reach a goal with a well-defined, pre-existing objective. Quilt University is a crazy quilt where bits or scraps or pieces of fabric get stitched together to find meaning in a messed up environment constructed out of chaos from participation in two environments—African American and dominant culture European America. Comparing the two gave me the beginning to look at a crazy quilt. The crazy quilt's contents were not written down in a structure that could be followed in Academic University. Piecing a crazy quilt consisted of odd minutes, varied patterns, and assorted colors sewn together into no set pattern except that it was joined to make a whole. Once the crazy quilt is completed the writing process can begin by reading the fabric and creating a text for writing in Academic University. This is what helped me to write the thesis. This understanding is significant because it creates histories, stories that are rooted in quilt history. It further gives the chosen fabric of individual lives.

I conclude by sharing that writing in Academic University has kept me sane. It has let me understand that I am a valid human being at the same time that I have received identity as well as a voice to speak with. I have gained the ability to learn from experience. The American philosopher John Dewey (1938) wrote:

> What avail is it to win prescribed amounts of information about geography and history, to win ability to read and write, if in the process the individual loses his own soul: loses his appreciation of things worth while, of the values to which these things are relative; if he loses desire to apply what he has learned and, above all, loses the ability to extract meaning from his future experiences as they occur?
>
> What, then, is the true meaning of preparation in the educational scheme? In the first place, it means that a person, young or old, gets out of his present experience all that there is in it for him at the time in which he has it. When preparation is made the controlling end, then the potentialities of the present are sacrificed to a suppositious future. When this happens, the actual preparation for the future is

CONCLUSION: PIECING SOCIETY

missed or distorted. The ideal of using the present simply to get ready for the future contradicts itself. It omits, and even shuts out, the very conditions by which a person can be prepared for the future. We always live at the time we live and not at some other time, and only by extracting at each present time the full meaning of each present experience are we prepared for doing the same thing in the future. This is the only preparation which in the long run amounts to anything. (p. 49)

In this work of the present I am grateful to my mentors and others who have pieced ideas in collaborative learning environments with me. I feel that here I have stitched something good and beautiful. It all seemed crazy in the beginning. However, after completing my crazy quilt and seeing the complete picture, it is not crazy after all. This is how curriculum is created and processed in Quilt University.

Afterword: Piecing as Democratic Pedagogy

By Lynne Hamer

One time early in our work together, I argued with Thelma Osbourne that something she had said didn't make sense to me. Thelma repeated her point several times, and then explained in patient exasperation, "You don't have to understand it. Just write it down." Osbourne's words deeply influenced me as a teacher educator and folklorist: it is in the act of valuing someone else's creation that we do our work. As teachers, we shouldn't let our self-centered desire to "understand" get in our way of valuing the bits our students bring, facilitating their bringing together old and new sources, extending our own understanding, and piecing together new knowledge and connections.

This piecing is the process of creating democratic culture. Rachel Davis Dubois, a pioneering intercultural educator of the 1920s through '40s, described intercultural education as creating democratic culture. She and colleagues developed a key method for this, "group conversation," which, she said, "deals with problems . . . which most democratic groups face at one time or another." Dubois explained:

> Basically, they are problems of communication, the kind of difficulties that imply a need for faith — faith in one's self, faith in the next person, faith in the group. What is needed is a kind of breakthrough, a reaffirmation of trust, a reconciliation with one's self, with each other, but even more with the unending possibilities for human growth and achievement which come with free, creative encounter. (Dubois and Li, 1963, p. 14)

Communication, faith, reconciliation, possibility. Dubois's description of (and instruction for facilitating) group conversation method sounds very much like Osbourne's description of the pedagogy of women's quilting for generations and centuries. Both Dubois and Osbourne emphasize the complexity of communication, the need for communication to develop trust in others, and the need to communicate with others in order to reconcile oneself with one's own past and thus to be able to grow and create. It is this third need that is, perhaps, less obvious and more surprising: that communication with others is necessary for *one's own* well-being.

In analyzing the power of intercultural education methods, the early psychologist of racism and prejudice Gordon Allport (1963) explained:

> All of us like to shuck off the burden of self-conscious reticence... We have a longing to be taken for what we are (whatever our racial or regional background); we want the security that comes from telling of our own cultures; we want to share the common coin of our humanity with others. (p. 10)

Significantly, Allport emphasized that this need is not unique to members of any one "racial" group. Osbourne likewise, while owning that for herself her experience is about being African American and a woman, emphasizes that the experiences of the metaphoric Quilt University are not only relevant for African American women, but are necessary for anyone, dominant culture or marginalized, to have in order to be fully functional in both their Quilt University and their Academic University. As Allport noted, "The participant does not think himself into a democratic way of acting (as lecturers, preachers, writers ask us to do), but rather acts himself into a democratic way of thinking" (1963, p. 11). With Quilt University, we can see how democratic culture is made, pieced purposefully together, in a learning environment that is purposefully constructed by its leaders— in the case of Quilt University, the elder quilters who have socialized, or taught, younger and newer members into their university for generations.

All of us, however, have sources of learning that we sometimes neglect to consider. Osbourne's work gave new importance to an early memory of my time in Quilt University, sitting under our family's dining room table on Mason Street in Omaha, Nebraska. I recall the legs of the table, forming an H-pattern, where I sat on the floor on one side of the crosspiece and looked across at my mother's legs, watching her right foot alternately push and release the pedal of her blue steel Singer sewing machine. I was sewing, too, with a needle and thread, scraps of the dress fabric that had fallen to the side, pieced with the light-brown tissue-paper pattern scraps that had fallen with them. I finished my quilt, crawled out from under the table and proudly presented it to her. She laughed joyfully, exclaimed on the unusual choices I had made for my piecing, and we both continued our work — hers on top of the table and mine comfortably under.

A dozen or so years later that same table stood in our dining room on North Second Street in Mankato, Minnesota. Along with more sewing projects, with both my mother and me using the machine on top of the table, I had watched my mother piece together bill payments and Christmas card lists on it, watched her assemble petitions to City Council, and helped her set the table for holiday dinners and party buffets. Once every two years I watched her piece together her book reviews for Thursday Reading Club, and each summer we used it to piece together my "demonstration" project for 4-H. In high school, I would sit at the table piecing together five-paragraph essays and once in a while a larger research report, while she popped in from the kitchen occasionally to see how I was doing, to suggest a stitch here, a piece there, a cut in between. After my junior year, it was college application essays. And then off I went, from then on to return physically to my Quilt University only for summers and holidays.

Educational theorist Madhu Suri Prakash described a different university, her mother's *rasoi*, or kitchen, with the word rasoi coming from the Hindi word *rasa*, a core word referring to the sacred:

> One of the many meanings of rasa is "juice" — the quintessential flow of flavors that comes only from slow, deliberate ripening that follows the organic rhythm of nature's cycles. rasoi literally means that sacred place in the home where these juices flow naturally, and therefore produce profound pleasure — for the palate, the eyes, and the soul. True artists in every field of creativity ... bring forth diverse and unique kinds of rasa. excellence of technique is necessary. but rasa only emerges when people combine the technical expertise that comes from the head, with habits of deepening the heart—connecting head and heart to the slow, deep workings of the soul. (2009, p. 49)

Prakesh spoke particularly of the connection between eating "slow cooked" food that they grew themselves and the development of character and creativity, but extended her call beyond food: "Ripeness of reform for the rasa of teaching and learning, living and eating is here.The time has come to regenerate the classical concept of 'school' — rooted in the Latin *schole*, or leisure" (2009, p. 50). Individuals grow and learn and create when our hearts and heads work together, and when we interact to bring learning and pleasure together.

Just as democratic interaction is the only way for individuals to grow and learn and create, it is also the only way for institutions to remain vital. Healthy schools grow and change constantly, in structure and in culture, as new people and ideas come into them, are combined with and react with established norms and knowledge, and result in renewed institutions of learning. It is this constant process of tradition and innovation, of old being used by individuals to create new, that constitute the "twin laws" of folklore (Toelken, 1996, p. 39) and the power of a folkloristic approach to schooling. And demonstrating how this is done is, I believe, Osbourne's great contribution to research in education.

Osbourne's *Quilt University* demonstrates how folklore can be used as the basis for successful formal schooling. The term "folklore" was coined in 1846 by Englishman William Thoms, who defined it as "the lore of the people" and described it as the material relics and oral material that seemed in danger of disappearing as England progressed into the industrial revolution (Bronner 2002, p. 9). The relationship that Thoms and others were describing at that time was the relationship between knowledge and production controlled by *the people*, versus knowledge and production controlled by *centralized authorities*— the government and capitalist institutions of production. Their fear was that as the latter became more prevalent, the former would become more marginalized and eventually would disappear. The larger fear was that in that process individual creativity would be destroyed and institutions of social life would decay and die.

The practice of quilting is certainly a folkloric one by any definition of folklore, but it is an activity that rather than dying out and disappearing, has become increasingly popular in many sectors of American culture including popular and elite— and folklorists including Pryor and Blake (2007) have specifically made quilting accessible as curriculum and aligned it with standards. In considering quilting, folklorists look at both folk process and artifact. In *The Study of American Folklore*, Jan Brunvand defined folklore as "the traditional, unofficial, non-institutional part of culture. It encompasses all knowledge, understandings, values, attitudes, assumptions, feelings, and beliefs transmitted in traditional forms by word of mouth or by customary examples" (1978, pp. 8–9). Quilting is all of these things: traditional, in that knowledge and skills are passed down intentionally and are recognizable from generation to generation; unofficial in that no one authority claims the right to tell others what to do and how to do it; and non-institutional, in that it takes place in many groups, all self-governing with their own ideals of what is good and bad, beautiful and flawed — whether in the quilting of fabric, or in the living of life. Significantly, for those of us who participate in formal schooling practices, folklore involves learning orally and by example — types of learning that are always present in, but not always valued in, schools, whether K-12 or university.

It is a small leap from this scholarship in folklore to seeing the relationship between the informal and non-formal education that occurs in households and neighborhoods, controlled by the people, versus formal education that occurs in schools, and is controlled by the elite in conjunction with market forces (Coombs & Ahmed, 1974). It is the informal education of home and community, along with the non-formal education of church and community organization, which constitutes people's knowledge, at its most basic: folklore (Hamer & Bowman, 2011). It is recognition of the value of this informal and non-formal education that Osbourne describes as basic to being able to participate successfully in formal education that occurs in schools — without in any way rejecting formal education. While harsher critics such as Prakash and Esteva (2008) have argued that "escaping education" is the only way for those who have been oppressed by Western institutions including schools to survive, Lucy Thelma Osbourne sees both informal and nonformal education, at home and learning within grassroots culture, Prakash and Esteva (2008) intensify the contrast between informal/non-formal and formal, in different terms: "Those classified and categorized as uneducated, underdeveloped, poor or undeveloped are struggling for their freedom from those who consider themselves to be educated or developed. Step by step, the former are dismantling all the institutions and projects of the latter which discriminate against them — including the educational enterprise" (p. 2).

In Osbourne's descriptive and analytic account of her own lifetime of learning, we see how she used her learning in Quilt University, the informal and non-formal settings where she learned from family and neighbors, as both a metaphoric and an explicit basis for her learning in the formal setting of the university. It is metaphoric in that it calls upon all of us to uncover and appreciate our own "universities," whether they are "fishing university" or "cooking university" or something else — and appreciate that learning as a potential framework for everything else we can learn. As Osbourne maintains, her experience is relevant to all students who have been shut out of the full opportunities provided by formal schooling — whether because of ethnicity, race, physical ability, gender, socioeconomic status, religion, or personal characteristics.

In the U.S., this line of understanding has been most developed by African American scholars, including W.E. B. DuBois (1903), who in his foundational work *The Souls of Black Folk*, described the phenomenon of "double consciousness" (p. 14). "Double consciousness" names the process whereby persons who have been taught they are inferior by the dominant culture must come to terms with the value of their own home cultures before being able fully to participate in the larger national scene. Aldridge (1999) claimed DuBois presents the basis for an African American philosophy of education, noting DuBois's call for African Americans to "ground themselves in their African and Negro culture before attempting to navigate within the larger society" (p. 370). This philosophy was further developed by Carter G. Woodson thirty years later as he critiqued the process of deculturalization, or "education under outsiders' control," as what happened to African Americans in formal schooling. Woodson warned, "If you control a man's thinking you do not have to worry about his action ... If you make a person feel that he/she is inferior, you do not have to compel him/her to accept an inferior status, he/she will seek for it" ([1933] 2011, pp. 23, 125). Woodson called for African Americans to "do for themselves" and become "autodidacts" — to rely on the informal and non-formal educational opportunities in their communities and of their making — that is, to cherish and grow from their quilt universities.

Drawing upon empirical research among indigenous groups in Mexico, Prakash and Esteva (2008) similarly noted "that those who become addicted to classroom instruction end up losing real opportunities for gaining the knowledge and skills with which communities endure and florish" (p. 6). It is Woodson's "do[ing] for themselves" and autodicatism, and Prakash and Esteva's "real opportunities" that Osbourne describes as Quilt University. But Quilt University does not reject Western formal schooling; rather, it requires piecing together scraps from all sources— family, church, community, school and university. And thus for Osbourne, all education — whether outside of schools and independent of cultural outsiders' (elite and popular culture) influence, or inside schools and controlled by elite and popular sources— is a matter of autodidactism: one must always piece one's own thesis.

Being able to draw on one's home learning as a basis for school learning has been shown over and over as essential for school success, and at the turn of the 21st century has been deepened to the level of basic pedagogical practices. In *Teaching Community*, bell hooks (2004) called for an "insurrection of subjugated knowledges" (p. 4), echoing John Dewey's (1929) argument by emphasizing that schools should be places where people learn something new to them, not just venerated culture, and noting that educators need to find and make spaces for teaching and learning outside the norm.

In her inspirational *Teaching to Transgress,* hooks (1994) exposed the nearly comprehensive requirement that university students abandon working-class home culture to succeed and described her ways of keeping that home culture alive and bringing it with her into the academy. Lisa Delpit's ([1995] 2006) classic *Other People's Children* captured the dilemma of removing schooling from local communities' control. Delpit described the different facets of cultural estrangement between teacher and students and depicted the efforts of nondominant-culture teachers to bridge the disconnects. Again, Delpit's insight came from her own experience as well as scholarly research, and named a truth for all of us as students: we have to be able to relate to and be understood by our teachers. Gloria Ladson-Billings ([1999] 2009) described "successful teachers of African American students" as those who "honor and respect the students' home culture" (p. 157). Ladson- Billings' formulation of "culturally relevant teaching" is most essential for those students whose home cultures have been most disrespected, but relevant to all. *Quilt University* is deeply specific to Osbourne's own experiences as an African American woman growing up in the segregated South and moving to the prejudiced North, but it is also universal to all of us as we bring together our home learning with our school learning to become whole, integrated, multifaceted and knowledgeable beings.

Thus in *Quilt University*, Osbourne gives those who have not participated in Academic University a pattern and example for successful participation in the university. She demonstrates how any student can bring her or his indigenous knowledge into the school both in bits and pieces, and as a conceptual framework for piecing together something new to the academy. However, she also gives instruction to those of us who live in Academic University to help piece together an institution that serves as an environment where varied people can bring their diverse understandings, experiences, and sources of information together and create, together, a deep, connected understanding that is necessary for new knowledge and functional society.

Works Cited

Aldridge, D. (1999). Conceptualizing a Du Boisian philosophy of education: Toward a model for African-American education. *Educational Theory*, 49(3): 359-79.

Allport, G. (1963). *ABC's of scapegoating.* 4th ed. New York: Anti-defamation League of B'nai B'rith.

Bronner, S. (2002). *Folk nation: Folklore in the creation of American tradition.* Wilmington, DE: American Visions.

Brunvand, J. (1978). *The study of American folklore.* 2nd ed. New York: Norton.

Cameron, D. (1992). *Feminism and linguistic theory.* New York: St. Martin's Press.

Collins, P. (1990). *Black feminist thought: Knowledge, consciousness and the politics of empowerment.* Boston, MA: Unwin Hyman.

Dewey, J. [1929] (1964). American education and culture. In R. Archambault (ed.), *John Dewey on education: Selected writings* (pp. 289-94). New York: Modern Library.

—. (1938). *Experience and education.* New York: MacMillan Publishing.

Dubois, R., and Li, S. (1963). *The art of group conversation.* New York: Association Press.

DuBois, W. E. B. (1903). *The souls of Black folk.* New York: Penguin.

Ducey, C. (n.d.). Quilt History Timeline, Pre- History – 1800. International Quilt Study Center and Museum. Downloaded http://www.quiltstudy.org/.

Elsley, J. (1994). *The Color Purple* and the poetics of fragmentation. In C. Torsney and J. Elsley (Eds.), *Quilt culture: Tracing the pattern* (pp. 68-83). Columbia: University of Missouri Press.

—. (1996). *Quilts as text(iles) The semiotics of quilting.* New York: Peter Lang.

Ferrero, P., Hedges, E., and Silber, J. (1987). *Hearts and hands: The influence of women and quilts on American society.* San Francisco, CA: Quilt Digest.

Freeman, R. (1996). *Communion of the spirits: African-American quilters, preservers and their stories.* Nashville, TN: Rutledge Hill Press.

Fry, G. (1990). *Stitched from the soul.* New York: Button Studio Books.

Hamer, L., and Bowman, P. (2011). Introduction: Through the schoolhouse door. In P. Bowman and L. Hamer (eds.), *Through the schoolhouse door: Folklore, community, curriculum* (pp. 1-18). Logan: Utah State University Press.

Hillard, V. (1994). Census, consensus, and the commodification of form: The NAMES Project quilt. In C. Torsney and J. Elsley (Eds.), *Quilt culture: Tracing the pattern* (pp. 112-124). Columbia: University of Missouri Press

hooks, b. (1989). *Talking back: Thinking feminist, thinking black.* Boston, MA: South End Press.

—. (1994). *Teaching to transgress: Education as the practice of freedom.* New York: Routledge.

—. (2003). *Teaching community: A pedagogy of hope.* New York: Routledge.

Howard L. (1993). *Alice Walker and Zora Neale Hurston: The common bond.* CT: Greenwood Press. Jordan, J. (1981). *Civil wars.* Boston, MA: Beacon.

Kelley, M. (1994). Sisters' choices: Quilting aesthetics in contemporary African American women's fiction. In C. Torsney and J. Elsley (Eds.), *Quilt culture: Tracing the pattern* (pp. 49-67). Columbia: University of Missouri Press.

Kirshenblatt-Gimblett, B. (1983). An accessible aesthetic: The role of folk arts and the folk artist in the curriculum. *New York Folklore*, 9(3-4): 9-18.

Lave, J, and Wenger, E. (1991). *Situated learning: Legitimate peripheral participation.* Boston, MA: Cambridge University Press.

Lorde, A. (1984). *Sister Outsider: Essays and speeches.* Berkeley, CA: Crossing Press.

Lyons, M. (1993). *Stitching stars: The story quilts of Harriet Powers.* New York: Charles Scriber's Sons.

Peterson, E. (1992). *African American women: A study of will and success.* Jefferson, NC: McFarland & Company.

Pryor, A., and Blake, N. (2007). *Quilting circles—Learning communities: Arts community and curriculum guide grades K-12.* Madison, WI: University of Wisconsin-Madison and Wisconsin Arts Board.

WORKS CITED

Prakash, M., and Esteva, G. (2008). *Escaping education: Living as learning within grassroots cultures.* New York: Peter Lang.

Prakesh, M. (2009). Rajinder's remarkable rasoi: What my mother's village kitchen can teach American schools. *Yes! Magazine,* 49: 48-50.

Rich, A. (1976). *Of women born: Motherhood as experience and institution.* New York: Norton.

Sciapiro, L. In C. Torsney and J. Elsley (Eds.), *Quilt culture: Tracing the pattern* (pp. 112-124). Columbia: University of Missouri Press.

Showalter, E. (1989). "Common Threads." In *Sisters' choice: Tradition and change in American women's writing.* New York: Oxford University Press.

Smitherman, G. (1977). *Talkin and testifyin: The language of Black America.* Boston, MA: Houghton Mifflin.

Toelken, B. (1996). *The dynamics of folklore.* Logan: Utah State University Press.

Wahlman, M. (2001). *Signs and symbols: African images in African American quilts.* 2nd ed. Atlanta, GA: Tinwood Books.

White, J., and Congdon, K. (1998). *Travel boundaries and the movement of cultures(s): Explanations for the folk/fine art quandary.* Art Education, 51 (3): 20-24,41.

Woodson, C. [1933] (2011). *The mis-education of the Negro.* New York: Tribeca Books.

 QU Press
Toledo, Ohio

QU Press is an independent publisher with the mission to promote cultural democracy in schools by making available to educators methods and materials highlighting individual creativity, traditional knowledge, and intercultural dialogue.

Editor: Lynne Hamer, Ph.D.

For more information or to share your thoughts,
please contact the publisher,

QU Press
749 Hilltop Lane
Toledo OH 43615

email qupress@bex.net

phone 419-690-4757

www.ingramcontent.com/pod-product-compliance
Lightning Source LLC
Chambersburg PA
CBHW041544220426
43665CB00002B/28